Young Person's
Occupational
Outlook
Handbook

Seventh Edition

*Based on information from
the U.S. Department of Labor*

The Editors @ JIST

Young Person's Occupational Outlook Handbook, Seventh Edition
© 2010 by JIST Publishing

Published by JIST Works, an imprint of JIST Publishing
7321 Shadeland Station, Suite 200
Indianapolis, IN 46256-3923
Phone: 800-648-JIST   Fax: 877-454-7839
E-mail: info@jist.com   Web site: www.jist.com

Acquisitions and Development Editor: Susan Pines
Database Work: Laurence Shatkin
Assistant Editors: Darlene Divine and Judy Morrow
Cover and Interior Designer: Aleata Halbig
Proofreaders: Laura Bowman, Jeanne Clark

Printed in the United States of America

14 13 12 11 10   9 8 7 6 5 4 3 2 1

   Library of Congress Cataloging-in-Publication Data
Young person's occupational outlook handbook / editors@ JIST. -- 7th ed.
       p. cm.
   Includes index.
   ISBN 978-1-59357-743-8 (alk. paper)
  1. Occupations--Juvenile literature. 2. Job descriptions--Juvenile
literature. 3. Vocational guidance--Juvenile literature. I. JIST
Works, Inc.
   HF5382.Y58 2010
   331.702--dc22
                              2010006375

We have been careful to provide accurate information throughout this book, but it is possible that errors and omissions have been introduced. Please consider this in making any career plans or other important decisions. Trust your own judgment above all else and in all things.

ISBN 978-1-59357-743-8

About This Book

This book presents information on 260 major jobs. These jobs cover 90 percent of the workforce, and you are very likely to work in one or more of them during your life.

In looking over these jobs, you should consider each one that interests you. Remember that you are exploring job possibilities. The information will help you learn which classes to take and what additional training or education you will need to do that job. If a job requires more training or education than you think you can get, consider it anyway. You can finance an education in many ways, so don't eliminate any possibility too soon.

The introduction gives you useful information to understand and use the book for career exploration. We hope this book will help you identify new jobs and new possibilities to think about.

We wish you a happy and successful future.

Contents at a Glance

Table of Contents

Professional & Related Occupations 49

Service Occupations 155

Sales & Related Occupations 183

Installation, Maintenance & Repair Occupations ... 237

Production Occupations.......................................**255**

Transportation & Material Moving Occupations.....277

Job Opportunities in the Armed Forces 287

Appendix: More Job Information on the Web 289

Index of Job Titles 301

Introduction

This book is designed to help you explore a wide variety of jobs. This is important because your career choice is one of the most important decisions you will make in life. This book includes descriptions of 260 major jobs, including green occupations.

The job descriptions answer questions such as these:

- What do people in this job do all day?

- What training or education will I need to do the job?

- How much does the job pay?

- Will the job be in demand in the future?

- What classes should I take now to prepare me for this job?

- What jobs are related to this one?

The information in this book is based on another book called the *Occupational Outlook Handbook (OOH)*. The *OOH* is published by the U.S. Department of Labor and is the most widely used source of career information. Like the *OOH*, the *Young Person's Occupational Outlook Handbook* groups similar jobs together. This makes it easy to explore related jobs you might not know about. Because the job descriptions in the *OOH* are more detailed than the ones in this book, you can refer to the *OOH* for more information on jobs that interest you. The information on green jobs was researched and written by the Editors at JIST Publishing.

Tips to Identify Jobs That Interest You

The table of contents lists all the jobs in this book, arranged into groups of similar jobs. Look through the list and choose one or more of the job groups that sound most interesting to you. Make a list of the jobs that interest you, and then read the descriptions for those jobs.

Information in Each Job Description

Each job description in this book uses the same format with eight sections:

On the Job: This section has a short description of the duties for the job.

Subjects to Study: Here you'll find some high school courses that will help you prepare for the job.

Discover More: This section has either an activity you can do to learn more about the job or a place to go for more information.

Related Jobs: This section lists similar jobs you can consider.

Something Extra: This box has interesting, fun facts or stories related to the job.

Education & Training: This section tells you the education and training levels most employers expect for someone starting out in the job. Almost all jobs require a high school diploma, so we do not include "high school graduate" as an option. Instead, we list the *additional* training or education the average high school graduate needs to get the job.

Here are the abbreviations we've used for the levels of training and education:

Short-term OJT = On-the-job training that lasts up to six months.

Moderate-term OJT = On-the-job training that lasts up to a year.

Long-term OJT = On-the-job training that lasts up to two or more years.

Work experience = Work experience in a related job.

Voc/tech training = Formal vocational or technical training received in a school, apprenticeship, or cooperative education program or in the military. This training can last from a few months to two or more years and may combine classroom training with on-the-job experience.

Associate degree = Two-year college degree.

Bachelor's degree = Four-year college degree.

Master's degree = Bachelor's degree plus one or two years of additional education.

Doctoral degree = Master's degree plus two or more years of additional education.

Professional degree = Typically, a bachelor's degree plus two or more years of specialized education (for example, education to be an attorney, physician, or veterinarian).

Plus sign (+) = The plus sign indicates that you need work experience in a related job as well as formal education. For example, "Bachelor's degree +" means that you need a bachelor's degree plus work experience in a related job.

Earnings: Dollar signs represent the approximate range of average earnings for a job.

$ = $24,000 or less per year

$$ = $24,001 to $32,000 per year

$$$ = $32,001 to $45,000 per year

$$$$ = $45,001 to $65,000 per year

$$$$$ = $65,001 or more per year

Job Outlook: This tells you whether the job is likely to employ more or fewer people in the future.

Declining	=	Employment is expected to decrease.
Little change	=	Employment is expected to remain about the same or increase as much as 6%.
Average increase	=	Employment is expected to increase from 7% to 13%.
Above-average increase	=	Employment is expected to increase from 14% to 19%.
Rapid increase	=	Employment is expected to increase by 20% or more.

Using the Earnings and Job Outlook Information

Are lower earnings "bad" and higher earnings "good"? Is rapid growth in a job better than slow growth or a decline?

Many people do not consider jobs if the jobs have low earnings or are not projected to grow rapidly. But we think you should look at earnings and growth as just two of several factors when you consider your job options. Here is some advice for looking at these important measures.

Earnings Information

Median earnings for an adult worker in the United States are about $32,000 a year. A four-year college graduate has median earnings about $20,000 more than that per year. There is a clear connection between earnings and education, and it goes like this: The more you learn, the more you are likely to earn. But information on earnings can be misleading. Some people earn much more than the average, even in "low-paying" jobs. For example, some waiters and waitresses earn more than $50,000 a year, although the average earnings for these jobs are much lower. Likewise, some high school graduates earn much more than the average for four-year college graduates.

Earnings also vary widely for similar jobs with different employers or in different parts of the country. Finally, young workers usually earn a lot less than the average because they have less work experience than the average worker in the same job.

This book presents earnings information for the "average" person in the job. But you should remember that half of all people in any job earn more than average, and half earn less. So don't eliminate a job that interests you based only on its average pay.

Job Outlook Information

The U.S. Department of Labor, part of the federal government, collects job information from all over the country. The department uses some of this information to guess which jobs are likely to grow and which are likely to decline—and by how much. The most recent information projects job growth through 2018. Some jobs will grow faster than average. Others will grow slower than average. What's more, some jobs are likely to employ fewer people by 2018 than they do now.

But, as with earnings, job growth should be only one point you consider in planning your career. For example, jobs that employ small numbers of people may have rapid growth, but they won't generate nearly as many new jobs as a slow-growing but large field like "cashier." Don't eliminate jobs that interest you simply because they are not growing quickly. Even jobs that are "declining" will have some new openings for talented people because workers leave the field for retirement or other jobs.

Some Points to Consider

Choosing your career is one of the most important decisions of your life. By exploring career options now, you will be better prepared to make good decisions later. Here are some things you should consider:

Your Interests: Think about what interests you. Your hobbies, school subjects you like or do well in, sports and clubs, home and family chores, volunteer activities, and other things can be clues to possible careers. For example, if you play an instrument or like to listen to music, you might think about a job in the music industry.

Your Values: It is important to look for a job that lets you do something you believe in. For example, if you want to help people, you will be happier in a job that allows you to do that. Or you may be able to find a hobby or volunteer job that lets you do this outside of your job. Either way, it's worth thinking about.

Education and Training: How much education or training are you willing to get? Most better-paying jobs require training or education beyond high school. Most jobs require computer skills, technical training, or other specialized skills. It's true that more education often results in more and better job opportunities. So you might want to consider getting a four-year degree or technical training after high school. For now, you should consider any job that interests you, even if you aren't sure whether you can afford the training or education required. If you really want to do something, you can find a way.

Earnings: What you earn at your job is important because it defines what kind of lifestyle you can afford. Higher-paying jobs usually require higher levels of training or education and/or higher levels of responsibility.

Working Conditions: Would you like to work in an office or outside? Would you rather work by yourself or as part of a group? Do you want to be in charge? What kinds of people would you like to work with? Consider these issues in planning your career.

Satisfaction: You will spend thousands of hours working each year, and you will be happier if you are doing work you enjoy and are good at. Your interests and values give you important clues to possible jobs.

Skills: What skills do you have? What skills do you need for the jobs you want? What skills can you learn or improve with more training or education? The skills you have—and the skills you can develop—are important parts of making good career decisions.

Self-Employment: Did you know that 7 percent of all workers are self-employed or own their own businesses? Head to the library, and you'll find books and other information on this topic. If self-employment appeals to you, don't let anyone tell you "you're too young" to start learning about it.

Getting More Information

As you can see, you have many points to consider in planning your career. This book can help you find the jobs that interest you. But when you're done here, you'll want to get more information. After you decide which jobs interest you, here are some ways to learn more:

Check out the *Occupational Outlook Handbook:* The *OOH* has more thorough descriptions of most jobs in this book, so you should start there. It's available in the reference section of your library or at your local bookstore. It's online at www.bls.gov/oco.

Visit the library: You can find the *OOH* and many other career books at most libraries. Ask your librarian for help in finding what you want.

Talk to people: Find people who work in jobs that interest you and "interview" them. Ask what they like and don't like about the job, how to get started, what education or training you need, and other details.

Use the Internet: You can find a lot of career information online. Throughout this book, you will see suggested Web sites to visit. In addition, the appendix lists hundreds of useful Web sites.

Talk with your teacher: Ask your teacher for ideas on other sources of career information. He or she might be able to help you find more information in your school library or elsewhere.

Remember, this book is only the beginning of your search for the right career. Don't rule out any jobs because they seem out of reach or because they don't pay enough. Follow your dreams, do your homework, and you'll figure out how to get from here to there.

"All our dreams can come true—if we have the courage to pursue them."
Walt Disney

Green Occupations

Biofuels Production Workers

On the Job

Biofuels production workers operate, maintain, and manage facilities that produce useful fuels from plant matter. Biofuels processing technicians measure and load the raw material and additives into chemical-processing equipment. During the process, these workers control valves, pumps, engines, or generators. Technicians record data, collect samples, and monitor quality. As a last stage, they run equipment to extract the biofuels and byproducts. Managers oversee production, maintenance, and safety.

Subjects to Study

Math, algebra, chemistry, biology, computer science, electronics, English, geometry, mechanical drawing, physics, trigonometry

Discover More

Different plant materials can be used to make biofuels. Search online for three plants that can be converted to biofuels. Write them on a list. Compare your list to your classmates' lists.

Related Jobs

Engineering technicians, engineers, industrial production managers, stationary engineers and boiler operators

Education & Training
Associate degree

Earnings
$$$$

Job Outlook
Rapid increase

Biomass Energy Production Workers

On the Job

Biomass energy production workers operate and manage facilities that generate energy from recently living organic matter, such as wood, agricultural residues, and waste paper. Biomass plant technicians measure and preprocess the feedstock. They feed the biomass materials into a combustion chamber or into processing equipment. They operate valves, pumps, engines, or generators to control production. They calibrate devices or meters. Managers direct and monitor the work.

SOMETHING EXTRA

Biomass has surpassed hydropower as America's largest domestic source of renewable energy. California has the largest biomass industry, but recent growth has been concentrated in the central and southern states because of the availability of feedstocks. The U.S. Department of Energy projects a 14 percent increase in energy uses of biomass in a 10-year period ending in 2018.

Subjects to Study

Math, algebra, biology, chemistry, computer science, electronics, English, geometry, mechanical drawing, physics, trigonometry

Discover More

The plants that create biomass draw carbon dioxide from the air as they grow. Burning biomass releases carbon dioxide, so the net effect is carbon-neutral. List a few points on the environmental differences between burning biomass and burning coal for energy. For help, visit www.nrel.gov/learning/re_biomass.html.

Related Jobs

Biofuels production workers; industrial production managers; methane/landfill gas production workers; power plant operators, distributors, and dispatchers

Education & Training
Short-term OJT to Long-term OJT

Earnings
$$$$

Job Outlook
Above-average increase

Energy Auditors

On the Job

Energy auditors inspect buildings, mechanical systems, electrical systems, or industrial processes to determine their energy consumption. They use special tools to measure energy use and the amount of air leakage. Energy auditors analyze energy bills and prepare reports with recommendations for cost savings. They may suggest home energy improvements, such as attic insulation, window retrofits, and heating system upgrades.

SOMETHING EXTRA

You may think that utility companies want to sell more power so they can earn more money. However, they lose money when they have to build generating facilities that are needed only on the coldest days of winter and the hottest days of summer. That's why the utilities encourage energy conservation. Some employ energy auditors and offer low-cost energy audits.

Subjects to Study

Algebra, blueprint reading, chemistry, computer science, electronics, English, geometry, mechanical drawing, physics, trigonometry

Discover More

Conduct an energy audit of your house. With a parent's or other relative's help, gather recent utility bills, go to http://hes.lbl.gov, and fill out the online form. It asks about your home's heating system, appliances, windows, and insulation. Then it calculates how much you could save by making your home more energy efficient.

Related Jobs

Engineers; heating, air-conditioning, and refrigeration mechanics and installers

Education & Training
Voc/tech training to Associate degree

Earnings
$$$$$

Job Outlook
Above-average increase

Geothermal Energy Production Workers

On the Job

Geothermal energy production workers install and operate facilities that generate energy from heat within the earth. At a plant that generates energy from steam, technicians run the turbines, pipes, and electronics and protect them from heat and moisture. They monitor power production and adjust it to meet demand. At geothermal installations that output hot water for direct use rather than electric power, technicians operate heat exchangers.

SOMETHING EXTRA

Even a modest level of geothermal heat can be economically useful. In winter in most of the U.S., the air is considerably colder than groundwater, the water in a lake, or the soil only a few feet below the surface. With a heat pump, which works like an air conditioner in reverse, it is possible to concentrate the modest heat from these sources and use it to warm buildings and provide hot water.

Subjects to Study

Algebra, biology, chemistry, computer science, earth science, English, geometry, mechanical drawing, physics, trigonometry

Discover More

What do hot springs, geysers, and volcano eruptions have in common? What do they tell us about heat within the earth? Write a paragraph answering these questions. Add your thoughts about the earth's internal heat and how it could be used for energy.

Related Jobs

Industrial machinery mechanics and millwrights; industrial production managers; power plant operators, distributors, and dispatchers

Education & Training
Work experience

Earnings
$$$$

Job Outlook
Rapid increase

Hydroelectric Energy Production Workers

On the Job

Hydroelectric energy production workers run facilities that generate energy from the force of moving water. Technicians monitor the operation and performance of complex electrical, mechanical, and electronic equipment. They make adjustments and repairs. To keep moving parts running, the technicians change oil or hydraulic fluid. They take readings and record data.

SOMETHING EXTRA

The most common form of hydropower is created by damming a river. It is sometimes considered less green than other forms of renewable energy. The dam may obstruct fish migration and impede sediment flows. It may deprive downstream wetlands of natural flooding and submerge upstream ecosystems. But the generation of power does not emit fumes or use a nonrenewable resource. Some experimental forms of hydropower, such as buoys that generate power from wave action, are expected to have less impact.

Subjects to Study

Algebra, biology, chemistry, computer science, electronics, English, geometry, mechanical drawing, physics, trigonometry

Discover More

To get a feeling for the energy of hydroelectric power, fill two buckets with water and carry them up several flights of stairs. Consider that all the energy this took from you is released when you carry the water back down the same distance. Now think about the quantity of energy that's available when a dam raises billions of gallons hundreds of feet.

Education & Training
Work experience

Earnings
$$$$

Related Jobs

Industrial machinery mechanics and millwrights; industrial production managers; power operators, distributors, and dispatchers

Job Outlook
Average increase

Methane/Landfill Gas Production Workers

On the Job

Methane/landfill gas production workers operate facilities that collect gas from landfills and process it as a substitute for natural gas. Technicians run the gas-gathering equipment, which includes plumbing, mechanical, and electronic devices. These workers keep a data log to meet environmental requirements. They may be responsible for identifying gas leakages and testing groundwater to ensure that pollutants are not leaching out.

SOMETHING EXTRA

Landfill gas is not a renewable resource because garbage creates gas only once, as it is broken down by microorganisms. If not properly purified, landfill gas can emit mercury vapors and dioxins when burned. However, the landfill gas replaces natural gas that would have to be obtained by drilling. Also, the combustion of the gas for commercial use transforms the methane to a less-threatening greenhouse gas (carbon dioxide). This process creates fewer smog-causing pollutants than would be produced if unrefined gas was flared off at the landfill.

Subjects to Study

Algebra, biology, chemistry, computer science, electronics, English, geometry, mechanical drawing, physics, trigonometry

Discover More

Trucks deposit garbage in landfills. List three reasons why most people do not want to live near landfills. For help, visit www.epa.gov/landfill/faq-3.htm.

Related Jobs

Diesel service technicians and mechanics; industrial production managers; power plant operators, distributors, and dispatchers; stationary engineers and boiler operators

Education & Training
Short-term OJT

Earnings
$$$$

Job Outlook
Average increase

Solar Energy Production Workers

On the Job

Solar energy production workers install and maintain *solar photovoltaic* and *solar thermal* systems that generate electric energy or collect heat from sunlight. Solar photovoltaic technicians connect solar panels to wiring that carries generated current. Solar thermal technicians mount solar collectors. To distribute the heat, they install pipes, ducts, heat exchangers, and circulating pumps, and then connect the heating system to storage tanks and to sources of power and water.

Subjects to Study

Algebra, biology, chemistry, computer science, electronics, English, geometry, mechanical drawing, physics, trigonometry

Discover More

You don't have to be a technician to work in the solar energy field. Workers are needed in communications, sales, marketing, accounting, and business support. To see the variety of jobs in solar energy, look at the job openings listed at www.ases.org (click "JOBS").

Related Jobs

Construction managers; electricians; heating, air-conditioning, and refrigeration mechanics and installers; plumbers, pipelayers, pipefitters, and steamfitters

Education & Training
Voc/tech training

Earnings
$$$$

Job Outlook
Rapid growth

Weatherization Installers & Technicians

On the Job

Weatherization installers and technicians make homes and buildings more energy efficient. They inspect and test every part of the structure. They fix windows, insulate ducts, install storm doors, and upgrade systems for heating, ventilating, and air conditioning (HVAC). These workers suggest energy conservation measures, such as low-flow showerheads and energy-efficient lighting. They prepare cost estimates and answer questions about their recommendations.

SOMETHING EXTRA

Weatherization workers sometimes do more than save money for households. Sometimes they save lives, because many heat-leaking old buildings have other problems. A weatherization program conducted by a utilities company in Louisville found that 23 percent of the households served had gas leaks, 26 percent had inadequate draft for heaters, and 16 percent had high levels of deadly carbon monoxide. Weatherization workers who do HVAC work are trained to detect and fix these hazards.

Subjects to Study

Algebra, blueprint reading, chemistry, computer science, electronics, English, geometry, mechanical drawing, physics, trigonometry

Discover More

About one-third of the heat lost from homes leaks through windows and doors. Other pathways for heat loss are folding attic stairs, fireplaces, and clothes dryers. Take a notepad and inspect your residence. Do you feel drafts around doors or windows? List all the energy wasters you find.

Related Jobs

Construction laborers; energy auditors; heating, air-conditioning, and refrigeration mechanics and installers; insulation workers

Education & Training
Short-term OJT

Earnings
$$$$

Job Outlook
Above-average increase

Wind Energy Production Workers

On the Job

Wind energy production workers operate and manage facilities that generate energy from wind power. Project managers oversee the development of wind energy opportunities. Operations managers supervise existing wind farms, including personnel and maintenance. Service technicians fix malfunctions in electrical, mechanical, and hydraulic systems. Because wind turbines have many moving parts and are exposed to strong forces of nature, the equipment requires frequent service.

SOMETHING EXTRA

Unlike coal or oil, wind cannot be stored for later use. Neither can the power that it generates, at least with present technology. In places with many wind farms, such as Texas, high winds may generate so much power that some turbines need to shut down. The local system is overwhelmed. There's insufficient capacity to carry the power elsewhere. Improvements to the national grid are needed to prevent such problems and make full use of wind farms.

Subjects to Study

Algebra, biology, chemistry, computer science, electronics, English, geometry, mechanical drawing, physics, trigonometry

Discover More

Check out www.windpoweringamerica.gov. Study the wind maps to learn how wind energy installations have increased over time. Other maps rate the speed of wind across the country.

Related Jobs

Industrial machinery mechanics and millwrights; industrial production managers; power plant operators, distributors, and dispatchers

Education & Training
Voc/tech training

Earnings
$$$$

Job Outlook
Rapid growth

Young Person's Occupational Outlook Handbook, © JIST Works

Management & Business & Financial Occupations

Administrative Services Managers

On the Job

Administrative services managers work for large and small businesses and government agencies. They manage the services that keep organizations in business, including the mailroom, food, security, parking, purchasing, and payroll. In large companies, they may manage other workers. In small ones, they may be responsible for all of these services themselves. Facility managers plan and manage workplace facilities.

Subjects to Study

English, math, speech, computer skills, economics, business courses

Discover More

Divide your class into groups of four or five. Have each group take a turn planning and directing a class activity. Groups have to decide what supplies they need for their activity, who will bring them in, and how they will teach the activity. For example, you might teach your classmates to make paper fans or create an assembly line to produce gingerbread houses.

Education & Training
Bachelor's degree +

Earnings
$$$$$

Related Jobs

Cost estimators; property, real estate, and community association managers; purchasing managers, buyers, and purchasing agents; top executives

Job Outlook
Average increase

Advertising, Marketing, Promotions, Public Relations & Sales Managers

On the Job

These workers help businesses sell their products. Before a product goes on the assembly line, marketing managers decide whether it will sell and who will buy it. Advertising managers decide what type of ads will work best. Promotions managers design campaigns to let the public know about the product. Sales managers direct the sales efforts. Public relations managers help companies create a good image.

SOMETHING EXTRA

Did you know that it costs on average $3,000,000 to run a 30-second television ad during the Super Bowl? That's about $100,000 per second that companies spend trying to convince you to buy their products. Imagine spending millions of dollars on something that people might not see because they've gone to get more chips. Now you know why advertising and marketing managers try so hard to be clever to keep your attention (and keep you from changing the channel).

Subjects to Study

English, speech, journalism, art, computer skills, business courses

Discover More

Closely study the commercials or ads you see. Some are funny, some are serious, others are just confusing. Are they effective? Do they make you want to buy the products they are promoting? How would you change an ad to make it more effective?

Education & Training
Bachelor's degree +

Related Jobs

Actors, producers, and directors; advertising sales agents; artists and related workers; authors, writers, and editors; demonstrators and product promoters; market and survey researchers; models; public relations specialists; sales representatives, wholesale and manufacturing

Earnings
$$$$$

Job Outlook
Average increase

Computer & Information Systems Managers

On the Job

Computer and information systems managers plan and direct technology in large and small companies and for the government. They hire computer programmers and support specialists. They manage the work and help determine salaries. They decide what workers and equipment are needed to do certain jobs. Often they are involved in the maintenance and security.

SOMETHING EXTRA

What do you think of when you hear the word security? An alarm, barred windows, maybe a guard (or at least a mean-looking dog)? In business, the biggest security threat often is to computer networks and the information they store. American companies spend billions each year on network security, often paying computer scientists to hack their systems—that is, to break into the company's network so that the in-house team can see the system's weak points and correct them.

Subjects to Study

Math, physics, chemistry, computer science, speech, business courses

Discover More

Take a tour of your school's computer lab. Does the lab instructor keep the computers in running order, or does the school use an outside contractor for that job? How often are the computers updated? Are they checked automatically for viruses?

Related Jobs

Computer network, systems, and database administrators; computer scientists; computer software engineers and computer programmers; computer support specialists; computer systems analysts; engineering and natural sciences managers

Education & Training
Bachelor's degree +

Earnings
$$$$$

Job Outlook
Above-average increase

Construction Managers

On the Job

Construction managers plan and direct construction projects. On small projects, they are responsible for all the people, materials, and equipment at a job site. They hire and schedule workers, make sure materials are delivered on time, and oversee safety. They often work outdoors and may be on call 24 hours a day to deal with delays, bad weather, and emergencies.

SOMETHING EXTRA

Did you ever wonder how builders choose what materials to use? Sometimes the environment decides for them. In China, for example, builders use stone and brick for construction because much of the land is treeless. In Northern California, builders cannot use wood-shingled roofs on houses because of fire hazard. In Mexico, houses are often built from mud bricks called adobe, which keeps them cool in the hot sun.

Subjects to Study

Math, shop courses, computer skills, drafting, business courses

Discover More

Taking shop courses at school, building small projects at home, and apprenticing with a skilled worker are some ways you can learn more about the construction industry.

Related Jobs

Architects, except landscape and naval; cost estimators; engineering and natural sciences managers; engineers; landscape architects

Education & Training
Bachelor's degree

Earnings
$$$$$

Job Outlook
Above-average increase

Education Administrators

On the Job

Education administrators are the managers of schools, colleges, and universities. They develop programs, monitor students' progress, train teachers, and prepare budgets. They must communicate with parents, students, employers, and the community. They might be school principals, college presidents or deans, or school-district superintendents. Many education administrators begin their careers as teachers.

Subjects to Study

English, speech, computer skills, statistics, psychology

Discover More

Ask the principal or dean at your school if you can "apprentice" with him or her for a day, watching, asking questions, and helping out as needed. Does the workday end when school is out? Will you have to attend evening meetings? Which aspects of the job do you like or dislike?

Related Jobs

Administrative services managers; counselors; human resources, training, and labor relations managers and specialists; instructional coordinators; librarians; teachers—kindergarten, elementary, middle, and secondary; teachers—postsecondary; teachers—preschool, except special education; teachers—vocational

Education & Training
Bachelor's degree +

Earnings
$$$$$

Job Outlook
Average increase

Engineering & Natural Sciences Managers

On the Job

Engineering and natural sciences managers plan and direct research, development, and production in large and small companies and research labs. They hire engineers, chemists, and biologists. They manage the work in a business or lab and help determine salaries. They decide what workers and equipment are needed to do certain jobs. Most of them begin their careers as engineers or scientists and work their way up to managerial positions.

SOMETHING EXTRA

Engineering managers who develop products must be innovative and change with technology to meet consumer demand. Consider how developments in computing, nanotechnology, energy, bioengineering, communication, and materials affect the way engineering managers look at existing products and envision new ones. Imagine creating the latest smart phone! Engineering managers consider the needs and wants of the public and how to best fulfill them.

Subjects to Study

Math, physics, chemistry, shop courses, computer skills, English, speech, business courses

Discover More

Ask to shadow your school lab coordinator for a day or two. What kinds of jobs does he or she perform on a regular basis? This might include supervising other workers and volunteers, keeping track of chemicals and other supplies, and preparing workstations.

Education & Training
Bachelor's degree +

Earnings
$$$$$

Related Jobs

Agricultural and food scientists, atmospheric scientists, biological scientists, chemists and materials scientists, engineers, environmental scientists and specialists, geoscientists and hydrologists, mathematicians, medical scientists, physicists and astronomers, top executives

Job Outlook
Average increase

Farmers, Ranchers & Agricultural Managers

On the Job

Because of the chemicals and equipment used, farming and ranching are dangerous jobs. Farmers on crop farms work dawn to dusk through the growing season to produce the grains, fruits, and vegetables that feed the country. During the rest of the year, many work second jobs. On ranches, animals must be fed and watered every day and fences must be inspected regularly. Aquaculture farmers are responsible for raising fish. Farmers and ranchers must have good business skills, because many farms are still family owned and operated.

Subjects to Study

Life sciences, shop courses, math, business, computer skills

Discover More

Planting, tending, and harvesting your own vegetable or flower garden are good ways to learn about crop farming. To learn more about animal farming, you could raise a small animal through the 4-H program in your community.

Related Jobs

Agricultural and food scientists; agricultural workers; engineers; purchasing managers, buyers, and purchasing agents

Education & Training
Long-term OJT to Bachelor's degree +

Earnings
$$$$

Job Outlook
Declining

Financial Managers

On the Job

Financial managers work for all kinds of businesses. Many work for banks, credit unions, or insurance companies. They prepare financial reports and make sure the business pays its taxes and has enough money to operate. They watch over the cash flow, manage the company's stocks, and communicate with investors. They decide whether the business needs to borrow money, lend money, or invest in stocks and bonds.

SOMETHING EXTRA

Managing a company's finances is a huge responsibility. Not only do the company and its employees rely on you to manage the money, but the investors do as well. Sometimes the power given to financial officers gets abused. Fraudulent activity has resulted in the bankruptcy of companies and the loss of employee and investor savings, proving that with great power comes great responsibility.

Subjects to Study

Math, English, business courses, accounting, writing, computer skills, speech, foreign languages

Discover More

Learn more about investing in the stock market by checking out these sites on the Internet:

Planet Orange: www.orangekids.com

Kids' Money: www.kidsmoney.org

The Mint: http://www.themint.org/index.html

Related Jobs

Accountants and auditors; budget analysts; financial analysts; insurance sales agents; insurance underwriters; loan officers; personal financial advisors; real estate brokers and sales agents; securities, commodities, and financial services sales agents

Education & Training
Bachelor's degree +

Earnings
$$$$$

Job Outlook
Average increase

Food Service Managers

On the Job

Food service managers select and price the food on a restaurant's menu. They hire and train workers and manage staffing, payroll, and bookkeeping. They oversee the preparation of food, order supplies and ingredients, and make sure the restaurant is clean. Many managers work nights and weekends, often under stressful circumstances.

Subjects to Study

Math, English, business courses, nutrition, family and consumer sciences, psychology, accounting

Discover More

The best way to learn about the food industry is to work in it. Consider taking a summer job at a local restaurant waiting tables, busing tables, or washing dishes. You can talk to someone who works in a restaurant about what he or she likes best about the job.

Related Jobs

Gaming services occupations, lodging managers, sales worker supervisors

Education & Training
Work experience

Earnings
$$$$

Job Outlook
Little change

Funeral Directors

On the Job

Funeral directors, also called morticians or undertakers, prepare bodies for burial or cremation. When someone dies, they help the family plan the funeral, write the obituary notice, and handle the paperwork. Most are licensed embalmers. Funeral directors are also businesspeople: They prepare bills, keep financial records, and hire and manage a staff. Most work long, irregular hours.

SOMETHING EXTRA

More people are opting for cremation and sometimes choose unusual ways to deal with their ashes. Star Trek creator Gene Roddenberry's ashes were carried into space on the space shuttle; 1960s rock icon Janis Joplin's were scattered off the California coast; and John Lennon's were wrapped as a Christmas gift and delivered to his wife, Yoko Ono. Perhaps the strangest of all was author Hunter S. Thompson, who had his ashes blasted out of a cannon!

Subjects to Study

Business courses, English, biology, chemistry, psychology

Discover More

Take a class trip to a local funeral home. Ask the director about his or her job: Does the director do much counseling with grieving families? Does he or she also do embalming—preparing bodies for burial? Does the funeral home offer cremation services? Has the director had clients who have made unusual requests for their ashes?

Related Jobs

Psychologists, physicians and surgeons, social workers

Education & Training
Associate degree

Earnings
$$$$

Job Outlook
Average increase

Human Resources, Training & Labor Relations Managers & Specialists

On the Job

These workers find the best employees to match jobs in their company. They interview job candidates. They may travel to college campuses to find the best job applicants. They help to resolve conflicts among workers or between workers and management. They provide some employee training and are concerned with worker satisfaction.

SOMETHING EXTRA

Would you go to a job interview wearing your swimsuit? Would you bring a sack lunch and sit munching a salami sandwich during the interview? Would you come in curlers, fuzzy slippers, or rubber flippers? Probably not, but some people do. Human resources managers interview all kinds of people. Most show up in business attire, but some come dressed in unbelievable costumes to get the attention of an employer.

Subjects to Study

English, business courses, psychology, sociology, communication skills, writing, computer skills, foreign languages

Discover More

If your school has a conflict-resolution team, volunteer to participate. If it does not, set up a team in your classroom. The team's job is to help out when two students have a dispute. Team members hear both sides and come up with a fair solution. They might teach conflict-resolution skills to other students.

Related Jobs

Counselors, education administrators, lawyers, psychologists, public relations specialists, social and human service assistants, social workers

Education & Training
Bachelor's degree to Bachelor's degree +

Earnings
$$$$

Job Outlook
Rapid increase

Industrial Production Managers

On the Job

These workers direct scheduling, staffing, equipment, quality control, and inventory in factories. Their main job is to get goods produced on time and within budget. They decide what equipment and workers use and in what order. They monitor the production run to make sure it stays on schedule and to fix any problems.

SOMETHING EXTRA

You have to have 10,000 widgets ready by Wednesday. Your widget painter cannot run at the same time as your widget packer. Your widget tops are arriving tomorrow, but the bottoms won't be in until the next day. Your widget-assembling workers charge double time if they have to work nights (and don't even think about asking widget workers to work on weekends). You must decide the best way to run the assembly line, when to run each machine, and whether to have your workers work overtime. And you must decide it all by noon. You're a production manager!

Subjects to Study

Math, English, shop courses, computer skills, business courses

Discover More

Plan an assembly-line process for making a craft. How many workers do you need? What materials and equipment will you use? How long will it take to make the item? How much will it cost? A manager must answer these questions.

Related Jobs

Advertising, marketing, promotions, public relations, and sales managers; construction managers; engineers; management analysts; operations research analysts; top executives

Education & Training
Work experience

Earnings
$$$$$

Job Outlook
Declining

Lodging Managers

On the Job

Lodging managers hire, train, and supervise the people who work in hotels, motels, and bed-and-breakfast inns. They set room rates, handle billing, order food and supplies, and oversee the day-to-day operations. Managers who work for hotel chains may organize and staff a new hotel, refurbish an older one, or reorganize one that is not operating well. Most work more than 40 hours a week, often at night and on weekends.

Subjects to Study

English, foreign languages, business courses, math, accounting, computer skills

Discover More

Call a local hotel and ask if you can "shadow" the front desk manager for a day. Ask about job responsibilities. What hours are required? How does the manager handle unpleasant customers? What emergencies has he or she faced in the last year?

Related Jobs

Food service managers; gaming services occupations; sales worker supervisors; property, real estate, and community association managers

Education & Training
Work experience

Earnings
$$$$

Job Outlook
Little change

Medical & Health Services Managers

On the Job

Medical and health services managers—also called health-care administrators—plan, organize, and supervise the delivery of health care. They determine staffing and equipment needs and direct the public relations, marketing, and finances of hospitals, nursing homes, clinics, and doctor's offices. They may be in charge of an organization or one department. These managers earn high salaries, but they often work long hours.

Subjects to Study

Math, English, speech, writing skills, business courses, psychology, health

Discover More

To learn more about careers in the health-care field, try volunteering at a nursing home or hospital in your community. Many have volunteers who read to or visit with patients and make small deliveries.

Related Jobs

Insurance underwriters, social and community service managers

Education & Training
Bachelor's degree +

Earnings
$$$$$

Job Outlook
Above-average increase

Property, Real Estate & Community Association Managers

On the Job

Property and real estate managers oversee apartment buildings, rental houses, businesses, and shopping malls. They sell empty space to renters, prepare leases, collect rent, and handle the bookkeeping. They make sure the property is maintained and respond to complaints from renters. Community association managers work for condominium or neighborhood owners' associations. Many of these managers spend much of their time away from the office.

Subjects to Study

Math, English, foreign languages, computer skills, business courses, accounting, shop courses

Discover More

Visit an apartment complex in your community and spend a day with the manager. Ask about the best and worst parts of the job, problems he or she sees in a typical week, and what kind of training you need for this job.

Related Jobs

Administrative services managers, education administrators, food service managers, lodging managers, medical and health services managers, real estate brokers and sales agents, urban and regional planners

Education & Training
Bachelor's degree

Earnings
$$$$

Job Outlook
Average increase

Purchasing Managers, Buyers & Purchasing Agents

On the Job

These workers look for the best merchandise at the lowest price for their employers or for resale. They find the best products, negotiate the price, and make sure the right quantity is received at the right time. They study sales records and inventory levels, identify suppliers, and stay aware of changes in the marketplace. Many spend several days a month traveling.

SOMETHING EXTRA

Were you born to shop? Do you love the mall? Are you a trendsetter? Buyers for department stores travel the world, attending fashion shows, visiting garment factories, and checking out small boutiques. They haggle for the best prices. When their work is done, they can stroll through the malls and see their choices on clothes racks, in store windows, and on other shoppers!

Subjects to Study

Math, business courses, economics, English, speech, computer skills

Discover More

Think of your family as a business. Help your parents compile a weekly supplies list. Then do some comparison shopping. Look online or visit several stores to see who offers the best prices. Will you save money if you buy in bulk? Should you buy from more than one source? How much can you save using coupons? See how much money you can save your family "business" in one week.

Related Jobs

Advertising, marketing, promotions, public relations, and sales managers; food service managers; insurance sales agents; lodging managers; sales engineers; sales representatives, wholesale and manufacturing

Education & Training
Long-term OJT to Bachelor's degree +

Earnings
$$$$

Job Outlook
Average increase

Top Executives

On the Job

Top executives make policies and direct operations at businesses and government agencies. They decide a company's goals and develop plans to achieve them. They meet with other executives, boards of directors, government heads, and consultants to talk about issues that could affect their business. They are responsible for the business's success or failure, so they are always under pressure.

SOMETHING EXTRA

Al Dunlap made a career of "rescuing" failing companies, often by eliminating thousands of jobs. He earned big money, but his methods earned him the nickname "Chainsaw Al." In the end, Chainsaw Al got hacked himself. When his company's stock fell, the board of directors fired the man who had made a career of firing others. Being a good top executive is about more than making a profit.

Subjects to Study

English, business courses, accounting, speech, computer skills, psychology, math

Discover More

You can learn more about being a leader by running for the student council at your school; taking a leadership position in a club; or planning activities at your school, church, or home.

Education & Training
Bachelor's degree +

Related Jobs

Administrative services managers; advertising, marketing, promotions, public relations, and sales managers; computer and information systems managers; education administrators; financial managers; food service managers; industrial production managers; lodging managers; medical and health services managers

Earnings
$$$$$

Job Outlook
Declining

Accountants & Auditors

On the Job

Accountants and auditors prepare and check financial reports and taxes. They work for businesses and banks, the government, and individuals. Some are self-employed, working as consultants or preparing people's tax returns. They use computers in their work.

SOMETHING EXTRA

In the 1920s, a gangster named Al Capone boasted that he owned the city of Chicago, and he was nearly right. The police seemed helpless to bring him down— until government accountants saved the day. Capone was finally convicted and imprisoned, not for the murders he ordered or the illegal drug-running he planned, but for the taxes he didn't pay.

Subjects to Study

Math, speech, business courses, economics, computer skills, accounting

Discover More

With your teacher's help, set up a banking system in your classroom. You can earn "class dollars" for good behavior, for turning in work on time, and for good attendance. You can spend those dollars on items from the "class store" or maybe on special privileges. Keep your bankbook up to date, recording each dollar you earn and each one you spend at the class store. At the end of each week, help your teacher perform an "audit" of the class's earning and spending.

Related Jobs

Bookkeeping, accounting, and auditing clerks; budget analysts; computer network, systems, and database administrators; computer software engineers and computer programmers; cost estimators; financial analysts; loan officers; management analysts; personal financial advisors; tax examiners, collectors, and revenue agents

Education & Training
Bachelor's degree

Earnings
$$$$

Job Outlook
Rapid increase

Appraisers & Assessors of Real Estate

On the Job

Real estate appraisers and assessors estimate the value of all kinds of property, from farmland to shopping centers. Their evaluations are used to help decide property taxes, mortgages, or whether property is a good investment for a client. They spend much of their time researching and writing reports, but they also get out of the office frequently to do on-site evaluations.

SOMETHING EXTRA

In some way, President Thomas Jefferson was acting as a real estate appraiser when he spent $15 million on a piece of land owned by the French in 1803. That piece of land stretched from the Mississippi westward to the Rocky Mountains, amounting to more than 500 million acres. The Louisiana Purchase, as it came to be known, doubled the size of the United States at the time. If the same land was purchased today it would cost $217 billion.

Subjects to Study

English, math, business courses, economics, geography, computer skills

Discover More

Do your own appraisal of your house or apartment building. Write down all of the features you see (such as a garage, fireplace, or patio) and note the condition of both the land and the building. Is the roof in good shape? Does the lawn need work? Write a report of everything you see that could be improved and show it to a parent or guardian.

Education & Training
Associate degree

Earnings
$$$$

Related Jobs

Claims adjusters, appraisers, examiners, and investigators; construction and building inspectors; real estate brokers and sales agents

Job Outlook
Little change

Budget Analysts

On the Job

Budget analysts help organizations decide how much money they need to run their business and how best to spend that money. They check reports and accounts during the year to make sure the business is staying within its budget and spending its money wisely. They look for ways companies can save money and use it more efficiently.

Subjects to Study

Math, business courses, economics, computer skills, statistics, accounting

Discover More

Imagine you are starting a business making widgets. Give yourself $10,000 to start, and then decide how to spend the money. Do you need employees? How much will you pay them? What equipment and supplies do you need? Do you have to rent work space? Make a budget for your business. Can you make a profit?

Related Jobs

Accountants and auditors; cost estimators; financial analysts; financial managers; insurance underwriters; loan officers; management analysts; tax examiners, collectors, and revenue agents

Education & Training
Bachelor's degree

Earnings
$$$$$

Job Outlook
Above-average increase

Claims Adjusters, Appraisers, Examiners & Investigators

On the Job

Insurance claims adjusters and claims investigators make sure that claims filed are covered by their company's policies. Then they decide how much should be paid and approve the payment. If the claim is not covered, they deny payment. Appraisers travel to see damaged property and assess how much the damage is worth. Sometimes investigators check out suspicious or unusual claims for fraud.

SOMETHING EXTRA

Sometimes people run away from their bills. This used to be called skipping out, which led to the term skip-tracing. Insurance investigators and collectors skip-trace people by checking with post offices, telephone companies, and credit bureaus. They may question family members, co-workers, and former neighbors. This job might not be dangerous, but it requires investigative skills.

Subjects to Study

Math, English, computer skills, economics, business courses, accounting, foreign languages, psychology, health

Discover More

Ask your parents if they have ever filed a claim on their car, home, life, or health insurance. Find out what they did to file the claim. Did they talk to an adjuster? Was the claim paid? Did their insurance rate go up?

Related Jobs

Accountants and auditors; bill and account collectors; bookkeeping, accounting, and auditing clerks; cost estimators; medical records and health information technicians; tax examiners, collectors, and revenue agents

Education & Training
Long-term OJT

Earnings
$$$$

Job Outlook
Average increase

Cost Estimators

On the Job

When a company is thinking about developing a new product, the owner needs to know how much it will cost to produce. What new machinery will be needed? How much will materials cost? How many workers will be hired? A cost estimator finds the least-expensive way to make the best product. Cost estimators decide what supplies to use, find the best prices, and estimate labor costs.

SOMETHING EXTRA

A company called a cost estimator to estimate the value of a load of scrap copper in the Mojave Desert. The manager warned the estimator that he might have trouble with the job. When the estimator arrived on site, he understood why. The company had been having such problems with thieves, it had dug a huge pit and set the copper inside. Then, for security, it had put rattlesnakes on top of the copper. The estimator peered into the pit, made his best guess, and high-tailed it home!

Subjects to Study

Math, computer skills, business courses, English, economics, statistics

Discover More

Plan a business making birdhouses from craft sticks. Decide how many birdhouses you will make, and then calculate the cost of producing them. Include your materials (craft sticks, glue, and paint), supplies (how about a hot-glue gun?), and labor costs (what you pay your helpers). How much must you charge for your birdhouses to make a profit?

Related Jobs

Accountants and auditors; budget analysts; claims adjusters, appraisers, examiners, and investigators; construction managers; economists; financial analysts; financial managers; industrial production managers

Education & Training
Bachelor's degree

Earnings
$$$$

Job Outlook
Rapid increase

Financial Analysts

On the Job

Financial analysts help businesses decide how to invest their money safely and wisely. Financial analysts use spreadsheet and statistical software to analyze data and spot trends. They recommend whether to buy, hold, or sell investments.

SOMETHING EXTRA

Wise investing is often a matter of timing. Most people know the rule "buy low and sell high," but how low is low enough, and what if high goes even higher after you've sold it? Imagine those people who made major investments in September 1929, unaware that a month later it would come crashing down, ultimately resulting in the Great Depression. Now imagine the pressure of being a financial analyst and telling a company what to do with its money!

Subjects to Study

Math, English, business courses, accounting, computer skills, economics, foreign languages

Discover More

A good way to learn about investing is to do it yourself. Look through stock listings online or in the financial pages of the *Wall Street Journal*. Pick two or three stocks—ones that look like safe investments or ones that seem to be growing. Pretend that you've invested $1,000 in each, and then track them for a month. Will you make or lose money?

Education & Training
Bachelor's degree

Related Jobs

Accountants and auditors; actuaries; budget analysts; financial managers; insurance sales agents; insurance underwriters; personal financial advisors; securities, commodities, and financial services sales agents

Earnings
$$$$$

Job Outlook
Rapid increase

Insurance Underwriters

On the Job

How much should an insurance company charge for car insurance? That depends on how likely a customer is to have an accident. Using national statistics, underwriters decide whether a person applying for insurance is a good risk. They help the company decide how much to charge. If they set the rates too low, the company will lose money; too high, and the company will lose business to competitors.

SOMETHING EXTRA

Are you a high-risk driver—or will you be? If you're under 21, your insurance company probably thinks so. Here's why. Underwriters look at accident statistics from all over the country to decide which drivers are most likely to be involved in accidents. They use this information to create a profile of a high-risk driver. People under 21 and those over 70 are two of the highest risk groups. It won't help if you drive a red sports car—just so you know.

Subjects to Study

Math, statistics, economics, English, business courses, accounting

Discover More

Talk with an insurance agent in your community. Ask about the company's rates. Are rates higher for those under 21? Are there other groups the company considers high risk? Do people who live downtown pay higher rates than those in the suburbs? Are rates higher for people who own sports cars? Why?

Related Jobs

Accountants and auditors; actuaries; budget analysts; claims adjusters, appraisers, examiners, and investigators; cost estimators; credit analysts; financial managers; insurance sales agents; loan officers

Education & Training
Bachelor's degree

Earnings
$$$$

Job Outlook
Declining

Loan Officers

On the Job

When you apply for a loan, you must provide information on your work, your assets and debts, and your credit rating. A loan officer will meet with you and help you fill out the application. Then he or she looks through your information and helps the bank decide whether to loan you the money; that is, the loan officer tries to predict whether you will pay it back.

Subjects to Study

Math, accounting, English, speech, computer skills, business courses, psychology

Discover More

Ask for a loan application from your parents' bank or credit union. Fill it out completely, including all of your sources of income, your savings, and your debts. Are you a good credit risk? Would you loan yourself money? Will your parents loan you money? At what interest rate?

Related Jobs

Financial analysts; insurance sales agents; insurance underwriters; personal financial advisors; real estate brokers and sales agents; securities, commodities, and financial services sales agents

Education & Training
Moderate-term OJT

Earnings
$$$$

Job Outlook
Average increase

Management Analysts

On the Job

Companies hire management analysts to solve problems. The work varies with each client and from project to project. When a management team realizes there is a problem, it may call in a consultant to collect and review information, figure out where and why the problem is happening, and decide how to fix it. The job may require frequent traveling.

SOMETHING EXTRA

Do you have what it takes to be a consultant? Many consultants are self-employed. They work on contract for a business, helping managers find the best way to solve a problem or make a product. When their work is done, they move on to the next client. Consultants must be detail-oriented, independent, and more than a little opinionated. They also should enjoy working on their own.

Subjects to Study

English, math, business courses, economics, accounting, journalism, speech

Discover More

Many consultants are self-employed. Interview people you know who are self-employed. How do they find their clients? Do they advertise? What do they like and dislike about being self-employed?

Related Jobs

Accountants and auditors; administrative services managers; advertising, marketing, promotions, public relations, and sales managers; budget analysts; computer scientists; computer systems analysts; cost estimators; economists; financial analysts; financial managers; human resources, training, and labor relations managers and specialists; industrial production managers; market and survey researchers; operations research analysts; personal financial advisors; top executives

Education & Training
Bachelor's degree +

Earnings
$$$$$

Job Outlook
Rapid increase

Meeting & Convention Planners

On the Job

These planners are responsible for ensuring that meetings and conventions come off without a hitch. They coordinate every detail: arranging speakers and locations, acquiring the necessary equipment, and dealing with problems. They interact with a variety of people and must have good communication skills. The job is fast paced and requires a great deal of energy and sharp organization skills.

SOMETHING EXTRA

Coordinating a meeting of 10 people is one thing, but planning a huge convention is a monumental task. For example, more than a million people attend the annual Chicago Auto Show, where new cars are showcased for the coming year. Such conventions are not only important for the attendees, but also for area hotels and restaurants that are more than happy to provide those people with places to sleep and eat.

Subjects to Study

English, math, business courses, speech, foreign languages

Discover More

Ask your teacher whether you can plan the next class function, or ask your parents whether you can plan their next party or social event. Draw up a schedule of activities and a list of resources you will need (food, beverages, entertainment, decorations). Coordinate every aspect of the event from the guest list to name tags and see whether you can plan a successful gathering.

Related Jobs

Food service managers; lodging managers; public relations specialists; travel agents

Education & Training
Bachelor's degree

Earnings
$$$

Job Outlook
Above-average increase

Personal Financial Advisors

On the Job

Personal financial advisors help clients with their financial needs. Advisors provide guidance on investments for retirement savings, education expenses, and other goals. They may be licensed to buy and sell stocks and bonds. Many advisors give tax advice or sell insurance.

SOMETHING EXTRA

Many clients trusted Bernie Madoff with their finances. Through word-of-mouth, Madoff attracted rich and famous people to invest through his firm. But Madoff turned out to be a fraud. He lost the life savings of his investors while living in luxury. His clients and the public were outraged. At age 71, Madoff was sentenced to 150 years in prison.

Subjects to Study

Math, English, business courses, accounting, computer skills, economics

Discover More

Ask your parents whether they have investments. If so, how did they make their investment decisions? What are their investment goals?

Related Jobs

Accountants and auditors; actuaries; budget analysts; financial analysts; financial managers; insurance sales agents; insurance underwriters; real estate brokers and sales agents; and securities, commodities, and financial services sales agents

Education & Training
Bachelor's degree

Earnings
$$$$$

Job Outlook
Rapid increase

Tax Examiners, Collectors & Revenue Agents

On the Job

Tax examiners, collectors, and revenue agents work for federal, state, and local governments. They review tax returns to make sure people and businesses are paying the right amount, send notices to those who have made mistakes, and track down those who are trying to avoid taxes. Most work 40-hour weeks, except during tax season when overtime is common.

SOMETHING EXTRA

As far back as ancient Egypt, governments have been collecting taxes. Most ancient books, including the Torah, the Bible, and Hindu Sutras, mention paying taxes. Some kings collected animals, crops, or slaves from taxpayers. Later governments demanded gold or jewels. Today, the IRS accepts money orders, personal checks, charge cards, or electronic fund transfers—but no sheep or corn!

Subjects to Study

Math, business courses, accounting, computer skills, English, foreign languages

Discover More

From January until April, your local library stocks tax forms of all kinds. Pick up a 1040 EZ form and ask your parents or a teacher to help you fill it out based on your allowance or job earnings. Read through all of the deductions carefully—you never know which ones you will qualify for!

Related Jobs

Accountants and auditors, budget analysts, cost estimators, financial analysts, financial managers, loan officers, personal financial advisors

Education & Training
Bachelor's degree

Earnings
$$$$

Job Outlook
Average increase

Professional & Related Occupations

Actuaries

On the Job

Actuaries analyze risk. Most of them design insurance plans that will help their company make a profit. They study statistics and social trends to decide how much money an insurance company should charge for an insurance policy. They then predict the amount of money an insurance company will have to pay to its customers for claims. Some actuaries are self-employed and work as consultants.

SOMETHING EXTRA

Because of their knowledge of insurance, actuaries are often called as expert witnesses in lawsuits. For example, they might testify about the expected lifetime earnings of a person who was disabled or killed in an accident. This testimony is used to determine how much money an insurance company must pay the individual's family.

Subjects to Study

Math, English, calculus, accounting, computer science

Discover More

Take a survey in your class. How many of your classmates have broken a bone or sprained an ankle? How many have stayed overnight in a hospital? How many have had their tonsils or appendix removed? Now separate the answers by boys and girls. Which group has had more medical emergencies? That's the group you would charge more for insurance.

Related Jobs

Accountants and auditors, budget analysts, economists, financial analysts, insurance underwriters, market and survey researchers, mathematicians, personal financial advisors, statisticians

Education & Training
Bachelor's degree +

Earnings
$$$$$

Job Outlook
Rapid increase

Computer Network, Systems & Database Administrators

On the Job

Computer network and systems administrators design, install, and maintain an organization's computer systems. They work with hardware and software, maintain efficiency, and analyze problems. Database administrators find ways to organize and store data. Because many databases are connected to the Internet, database administrators must coordinate security with network administrators. These workers do their jobs in businesses, labs, and government organizations.

SOMETHING EXTRA

The demand for network and systems administrators will increase as firms invest in new technologies. The growth of mobile technology means that even more companies will use the Internet to do business online. Companies need systems administrators who can use technology to communicate with employees, clients, and consumers. As cyber attacks become more sophisticated, demand will rise for workers with information security skills.

Subjects to Study

Computer science, math, shop and technology courses, statistics

Discover More

Ask your computer lab or media center specialist to show you the ways they back up the information in the school's computers. Some save the data onto other computers or through an online backup service. Others may use external hard drives or writable CDs to store material.

Education & Training
Associate to Bachelor's degree

Earnings
$$$$$

Related Jobs

Computer and information systems managers, computer scientists, computer software engineers and computer programmers, computer support specialists, computer systems analysts

Job Outlook
Rapid increase

Computer Scientists

On the Job

Computer scientists are researchers and inventors. Some work for universities, while others work for research companies. Many work on cutting-edge technology such as virtual reality or robot design. Scientists who research hardware architecture discover new ways for computers to process information. They design computer chips and processors that are faster and more powerful.

Subjects to Study

Computer science, math, shop and technology courses, statistics

Discover More

Did you know your computer gives out radio waves? Try this experiment and see. Get a small radio and set it on AM. Turn it on and find a spot between stations so that you just receive static. Now turn the radio up high and put it next to your computer. You should hear sounds from your computer on the radio!

Education & Training
Doctoral degree

Earnings
$$$$$

Related Jobs

Computer and information systems managers; computer network, systems, and database administrators; computer software engineers and computer programmers; computer support specialists; engineers; teachers—postsecondary

Job Outlook
Rapid increase

Computer Software Engineers & Computer Programmers

On the Job

Computer software engineers do research, design computers and programs, and find new ways to use them in business. They may identify problems in business, science, and engineering and then design specialized computer software to solve those problems.

SOMETHING EXTRA

Do you like to play computer games like Super Mario Kart, The Sims, or maybe Final Fantasy? Did you ever wonder who makes up games like these? Computer programmers create them. Programmers work for computer game publishers, writing new games and adding new twists to old games, all of them hoping to create the next big hit.

Computer programmers write, update, test, and maintain the software that makes computers work. They provide step-by-step instructions for the computer.

Subjects to Study

Math, physics, computer science, communication skills, electronics, shop and technology courses

Discover More

The image you see on a computer monitor is made up of thousands of tiny dots. Color monitors use red, green, and blue dots. Use a magnifying glass to look at the screen, or use a drop of water to act like a lens. Get a tiny drop of water on your finger tip and touch it to your computer screen. (Be careful not to drip!) Do you see the dots?

Education & Training
Bachelor's degree

Earnings
$$$$$

Related Jobs

Actuaries; computer network, systems, and database administrators; computer scientists; computer support specialists; computer systems analysts; engineers; mathematicians; operations research analysts; statisticians

Job Outlook
Rapid increase

Computer Support Specialists

On the Job

What happens when a company's computers suddenly begin crashing? They call in the support specialist, the troubleshooters of the computer world. These workers find and fix problems for businesses and individual computer owners. Specialists work in organizations, for computer hardware or software vendors, or for organizations that provide support services on a contract basis, such as help-desk service firms.

SOMETHING EXTRA

Networking links all the computers in a company so that workers using computers can trade information. It allows people to communicate by e-mail—a major convenience and a major worry for businesses. As more workers are linked online, more time is wasted trading jokes, recipes, videos, photos, and gossip. It has been estimated that companies lose $54 billion per year in worker productivity related to e-mail, social media, and Web surfing.

Subjects to Study

Math, computer science, shop and technology courses

Discover More

Call the tech support hotline for a computer company. (Ask your parents first; these calls may cost money, and many are long distance.) Ask how the support person can fix a computer problem over the phone.

Related Jobs

Broadcast and sound engineering technicians and radio operators; computer and information systems managers; computer network, systems, and database administrators; computer software engineers and computer programmers; customer service representatives

Education & Training
Associate degree

Earnings
$$$

Job Outlook
Above-average increase

Computer Systems Analysts

On the Job

Computer systems analysts are primarily responsible for assessing and meeting the technology needs of other businesses. They help businesses and organizations decide what computer systems will best help them grow or solve their problems. They often set up and test the new technology as well.

SOMETHING EXTRA

Computer software and hardware often becomes outdated almost as soon as you buy it. The average life span for a personal computer is three to five years, and nearly 6,000 computers become obsolete every day in California alone. Computer systems analysts have to be aware of these changes in technology so they can keep businesses on the cutting edge.

Subjects to Study

Math, physics, computer science, business courses, shop and technology courses

Discover More

Research the specifications and features of your computer at school or at home. How fast is the processor? How much RAM does it have? How big is the hard drive? What operating system is it running? Now compare it to one of the more expensive computers that just came on the market to see how outdated it is.

Related Jobs

Actuaries; computer and information systems managers; computer network, systems, and database administrators; computer software engineers and computer programmers; engineers; management analysts; mathematicians; operations research analysts; statisticians

Education & Training
Bachelor's degree

Earnings
$$$$$

Job Outlook
Rapid increase

Mathematicians

On the Job

Mathematicians work in two areas: theory and applications. Theoretical mathematicians look for relationships between new math principles and old ones. This can help in science and engineering. Applied mathematicians use math to solve problems in business, government, and everyday life. Many mathematicians teach at colleges and universities.

Subjects to Study

Algebra, geometry, trigonometry, calculus, logic, computer science, physics, statistics

Discover More

To try your hand at some fun and challenging math activities, visit the MathCats at www.mathcats.com or the Galileo gallery of math puzzles at www.galileo.org/math/puzzles.html.

Related Jobs

Actuaries; computer network, systems, and database administrators; computer scientists; computer software engineers and computer programmers; computer systems analysts; economists; engineers; financial analysts; market and survey researchers; operations research analysts; personal financial advisors; physicists and astronomers; statisticians

Education & Training
Doctoral degree

Earnings
$$$$$

Job Outlook
Rapid increase

Operations Research Analysts

On the Job

Operations research analysts help businesses run efficiently by applying mathematical principles to problems. First, analysts define and study the problem. Next, they gather information by talking with people and choosing which mathematical model they will use. Finally, they present their findings and recommendations to the company's management.

Subjects to Study

Math, statistics, computer skills, English, communication skills, logic, business courses

Discover More

Take a walk through your school building. Now, using graph paper, make a map of the building, including all the classrooms, offices, restrooms, cafeteria, and exits. Using your map, plot the most direct, effective way to deliver mail to each classroom and office. Then plot the most efficient exit route from each classroom.

Related Jobs

Computer software engineers and computer programmers, computer systems analysts, economists, engineers, management analysts, market and survey researchers, mathematicians, statisticians

Education & Training
Master's degree

Earnings
$$$$$

Job Outlook
Rapid increase

Statisticians

On the Job

Statisticians collect information from surveys and experiments. They decide where and how to gather the information, who to survey, and what questions to ask. They use the information they collect to make predictions about the economy or to assess social problems. This data helps business and government leaders make decisions. Because computers play such a big role in collecting and analyzing data, statisticians need to know as much about computers as they do about math.

SOMETHING EXTRA

How can a doctor tell whether a new medicine is safe to prescribe? How can a company tell whether people like one product more than another? How does the government know the unemployment rate? The answer to these questions is statistics. An agency surveys people, compiles the answers, and uses math formulas to tell what percentage of respondents reacts badly to a medicine, likes a product, or has a job.

Subjects to Study

Math, algebra, statistics, economics, business courses, sciences, computer skills

Discover More

The next time you go to a sporting event, take a notebook and pencil. Try to keep track of the statistics of one team or of key players. At the end of the game, add your figures and provide a summary of the team's or players' performance.

Related Jobs

Actuaries, computer scientists, computer software engineers and computer programmers, computer systems analysts, economists, engineers, financial analysts, market and survey researchers, mathematicians

Education & Training
Master's degree

Earnings
$$$$$

Job Outlook
Average increase

Architects, Except Landscape & Naval

On the Job

Architects design buildings and other structures. They make sure buildings are functional, safe, and economical. They draw plans of every part of a building, including the plumbing and electrical systems. They help choose a building site and decide what materials to use. Architects use computers in their work, and many are self-employed.

SOMETHING EXTRA

Architecture can be a tricky business. Take, for example, the bell tower for a certain cathedral in the Italian city of Pisa. Before it was completed (in 1174), it began to lean—which is why the top section is still kinked. The Leaning Tower of Pisa has been leaning for more than 800 years, and architectural engineers are still finding new ways to keep it propped up.

Subjects to Study

Math, English, drawing courses, drafting, computer science, shop and technology courses

Discover More

What does your dream house look like? Using graph paper, draw a room-by-room floor plan of your ideal home. Include all the elements you would like—maybe a fireplace, an exercise room, a game room, or a spa. Don't forget the practical rooms—everyone needs a kitchen and a bath!

Related Jobs

Commercial and industrial designers, construction managers, engineers, graphic designers, interior designers, landscape architects, urban and regional planners

Education & Training
Bachelor's degree

Earnings
$$$$$

Job Outlook
Above-average increase

Landscape Architects

On the Job

Landscape architects make areas such as parks, malls, and golf courses beautiful and useful. They decide where the buildings, roads, and walkways will go. They choose how the flower gardens and trees should be arranged. They create designs, estimate costs, and check that the plans are carried out correctly. They must make sure their designs are environmentally friendly. Some work for major companies, but many are self-employed.

SOMETHING EXTRA

In the days before computers, architects had to draw their landscape designs by hand. Today, they use computer-aided design (CAD) systems and video simulations to let their clients see their ideas in full color. Then, if the client wants to make a change, the architect can do it with the click of a mouse—saving time and money.

Subjects to Study

Math, botany, ecology, drafting, art, geology, computer skills

Discover More

Design a flower garden that will grow in your area's climate. What colors do you want? Should you use tall plants, short ones, or a combination? Do you want all spring bloomers or plants that will bloom at various times? How much maintenance will it need?

Related Jobs

Architects, except landscape and naval; construction managers; engineers; environmental scientists and specialists; geoscientists and hydrologists; surveyors, cartographers, photogrammetrists, and surveying and mapping technicians; urban and regional planners

Education & Training
Bachelor's degree

Earnings
$$$$

Job Outlook
Rapid increase

Surveyors, Cartographers, Photogrammetrists & Surveying & Mapping Technicians

On the Job

These workers measure and map the earth's surface to set official land, air, and water boundaries. They may check old legal documents for information and write reports. They work outdoors in all kinds of weather and may travel long distances to work sites. Cartographers use the information surveyors gather to prepare maps and charts. Photogrammetrists analyze aerial photographs to help make detailed maps.

SOMETHING EXTRA

Satellites have changed the way surveyors work. A GPS (Global Positioning System) uses radio signals from satellites to locate points on the earth. The surveyor places a radio receiver at the desired point, and the receiver can collect information from several satellites at once. Such a receiver can also be placed in a car and used to trace a road system. To think at one time we thought the world was flat!

Subjects to Study

Algebra, geometry, trigonometry, drafting, computer science, English, geography, geology, photography

Discover More

Make a map of your neighborhood, showing how to get from your house to your school. Include all streets and important landmarks, bodies of water or forests, malls or business districts, parks and playgrounds—anything that acts as a landmark in your area. If you gave someone at school your map, could the person get to your house?

Related Jobs

Architects, except landscape and naval; engineers; environmental scientists and specialists; landscape architects; social scientists, other; urban and regional planners

Education & Training
Moderate-term OJT to Bachelor's degree

Earnings
$$$$

Job Outlook
Average increase

Engineers

On the Job

Engineers design machinery, buildings, and highways. They develop new products and new ways of making them. Some engineers test the quality of products. Some supervise production in factories. They may work in laboratories, offices, and construction sites. Most engineers specialize in a particular industry or with particular materials.

SOMETHING EXTRA

Can you imagine a world without engineers? It's nearly impossible. Without engineers, we would have no bridges and dams, no interstate highways, no airliners or space flights, and no roller coasters or tilt-a-whirls at the amusement parks. Engineering affects almost every aspect of our lives, from home to work to play.

Subjects to Study

Math, physics, chemistry, shop and technology courses, drafting, computer skills

Discover More

You've probably made paper airplanes, but have you experimented with your design to increase their flight? Have you tried using heavier or lighter paper, or different kinds of glue? Have you cut flaps in the wings? Using different designs and materials, make five different paper airplanes and do test flights.

Related Jobs

Chemists and materials scientists, computer software engineers and computer programmers, drafters, engineering and natural sciences managers, engineering technicians, environmental scientists and specialists, geoscientists and hydrologists, mathematicians, physicists and astronomers, sales engineers

Education & Training
Bachelor's degree

Earnings
$$$$$

Job Outlook
Average increase

Drafters

On the Job

Drafters prepare the drawings used to build everything from spacecraft to bridges. Using rough sketches done by others, they produce detailed technical drawings with specific information to create a finished product. Drafters use handbooks, tables, calculators, and computers to do their work. Many specialize in architecture, electronics, or aeronautics.

SOMETHING EXTRA

Why are blueprints blue? Before computer-aided drafting, drafters would place their original drawing over special chemically treated white paper. A bright light was shone on the combined sheets of paper for several minutes, and then the special treated paper was placed in a developing solution. The result: The paper turned blue everywhere except for where the original tracing had blocked the light, creating a perfect negative image of the original drawing—a blueprint!

Subjects to Study

Math, physics, drafting, art and design courses, computer skills, shop and technology courses

Discover More

Try making your own drawing of a building or some kind of machine. You can use either paper and pencil or a computer drawing program. You can find books about drafting at the library.

Related Jobs

Architects, except landscape and naval; commercial and industrial designers; engineering technicians; engineers; landscape architects; science technicians; surveyors, cartographers, photogrammetrists, and surveying and mapping technicians

Education & Training
Voc/tech training

Earnings
$$$$

Job Outlook
Little change

Engineering Technicians

On the Job

Engineering technicians use science, engineering, and math to solve problems for businesses. They help engineers and scientists with experiments and develop models of new equipment. Some supervise production workers or check the quality of products. Like engineers, they often specialize in an area such as mechanics, electronics, or chemicals. Some may be exposed to hazards from equipment, chemicals, or toxic materials.

SOMETHING EXTRA

Manufacturing a product efficiently involves a lot of planning and testing. In 1895, King C. Gillette, a Boston bottle-cap salesman, came up with the idea of a disposable razor blade. He spent eight years developing the methods to mass-produce his product for sale to the public. Most Americans have used his invention at one time or another.

Subjects to Study

Math, physics, chemistry, electronics, shop and technology courses, drafting

Discover More

What's the simplest way to boil an egg? Easy, right? Just put the egg in a pan of boiling water and cook it. Now think about the reverse. How *complicated* can you make the job? On paper, draw an egg-boiling machine. Make it as complicated and ridiculous as you can.

Related Jobs

Broadcast and sound engineering technicians and radio operators, drafters, science technicians

Education & Training
Associate degree

Earnings
$$$$

Job Outlook
Little change

Agricultural & Food Scientists

On the Job

Agricultural scientists study farm crops and animals. They look for ways to control pests and weeds safely, increase crop yields with less labor, and save water and soil. Many work outdoors in all kinds of weather. Food scientists work in the food-processing industry, at universities, and for the government. They look for new food sources and preservatives and help ensure that our food is safe.

SOMETHING EXTRA

Will chickens hatch in space? Scientists wondered how the lack of gravity would affect hatching eggs, so they sent fertilized chicken eggs into space aboard the space shuttle. Some eggs did not survive the flight. Of the ones that survived, some eggs hatched. The space chickens returned to Earth safe and sound (the astronauts took enough other food supplies with them) to be studied further.

Subjects to Study

Biology, environmental science, physics, chemistry, math, business, life sciences, nutrition, family and consumer sciences

Discover More

Set up a growing experiment. Choose a plant and get a package of seeds at a garden center. Now plant the seeds in four containers. Put two containers on a sunny windowsill and two in a shady spot. Water one in the window and one in the shade every day. Water the other two once every four or five days. Which seeds grow best?

Related Jobs

Biological scientists; chemists and materials scientists; conservation scientists and foresters; farmers, ranchers, and agricultural managers; medical scientists; veterinarians

Education & Training
Doctoral degree to Bachelor's degree

Earnings
$$$$

Job Outlook
Above-average increase

Biological Scientists

On the Job

Biological scientists study living things and their environment. They do research, develop new medicines, increase crop amounts, and improve the environment. Some study specialty areas such as viruses, ocean life, plant life, or animal life. They may work in company, college, or government labs, or as high school biology teachers.

SOMETHING EXTRA

In 2002, a deadly new disease called SARS, or Severe Acute Respiratory Syndrome, began killing people in southern China. Because the disease was new, no vaccinations or medications could prevent or cure it. Because of air travel, the disease was spreading as far away as Canada. Biological scientists sprang into action and were able to identify the virus that causes the disease.

Subjects to Study

Math, biology, botany, chemistry, zoology, physics, computer science, environmental studies

Discover More

Study the effects of acid rain on plant life. Get two small potted plants from a garden center. Keep them in the same place. Water one daily with regular tap water. Water the other with "acid rain" you make by adding a half teaspoon of white vinegar to two-and-a-half teaspoons of tap water. Which plant grows better?

Related Jobs

Agricultural and food scientists, conservation scientists and foresters, dentists, engineering and natural sciences managers, medical scientists, physicians and surgeons, teachers—postsecondary, veterinarians

Education & Training
Bachelor's degree to Doctoral degree

Earnings
$$$$$

Job Outlook
Rapid increase

Conservation Scientists & Foresters

On the Job

Foresters and conservation scientists manage, use, and protect natural resources such as water, wood, and wildlife. Foresters supervise the use of timber for lumber companies. Range managers oversee range lands so that the environment is not damaged. Soil conservationists help farmers save the soil, water, and other natural resources.

SOMETHING EXTRA

In 1980, a volcano in Washington state called Mount St. Helens erupted, blowing off the entire north face of the mountain. The blast destroyed thousands of acres of forest and heated the ground so much that nothing grew for years. Rather than replanting, the U.S. Forest Service decided to leave the blast site alone, to watch how the mountain recovered on its own. Wildflowers and saplings are growing. In a hundred years or so, there will be a new forest.

Subjects to Study

Math, chemistry, biology, botany, ecology, agriculture, computer science, economics, business courses

Discover More

Foresters understand that for every tree that is cut down, a new tree must be planted. Ask your parents if you can pick out a tree from a nursery and plant it in your yard, taking into consideration the tree's needs for sunlight and space. Or talk to your teachers about the possibility of organizing a tree-planting event. For more information on how to plant trees, visit www.kidsface.org/pages/plant.html.

Education & Training
Bachelor's degree

Earnings
$$$$

Related Jobs

Agricultural and food scientists; biological scientists; environmental scientists and specialists; farmers, ranchers, and agricultural managers; geoscientists and hydrologists

Job Outlook
Average increase

Medical Scientists

On the Job

Medical scientists research human diseases to improve human health. Most medical scientists do basic research to learn more about viruses, bacteria, and infectious diseases. Then this information is used to develop vaccines, medicines, and treatments. While some medical scientists work in clinics or hospitals, most work in government, university, or private industry labs.

Subjects to Study

Chemistry, biology, math, physics, computer science

Discover More

Take a walk in the park and look for piles of leaves and fallen tree limbs and sticks. Notice that at the bottom of the piles, the leaves and sticks have started to crumble and fall apart. What causes this? Special microbes such as bacteria eat dead material such as leaves and sticks and turn it into a powder called compost. Take some compost home and put it on your houseplants or in your garden. Does it help your plants grow bigger?

Education & Training
Doctoral degree

Earnings
$$$$$

Related Jobs

Agricultural and food scientists, biological scientists, dentists, pharmacists, physicians and surgeons, teachers—postsecondary, veterinarians

Job Outlook
Rapid increase

Atmospheric Scientists

On the Job

Atmospheric scientists, commonly called meteorologists, study the atmosphere (the air that covers the earth) for its effects on our environment. The most well-known area of their work is weather forecasting. They also study trends in the earth's climate and apply their research to air-pollution control, environmental studies, air and sea transportation, and defense. Meteorologists often work nights, weekends, and holidays at weather stations.

SOMETHING EXTRA

Even with advanced warning from meteorologists, it is sometimes difficult to avoid destruction caused by Mother Nature. In 2005, Hurricane Katrina hit in Florida, Mississippi, Alabama, and Louisiana, with particularly devastating effects on New Orleans. Killing at least 1,600 people and doing $75 billion in damage, it is considered the most destructive hurricane in American history.

Subjects to Study

Math, chemistry, physics, computer science, statistics, environmental science

Discover More

Contact a local TV station and ask to become one of its weather watchers. Hang a thermometer outside—a little way away from your home. Take daily readings. Place a large, rimmed dish on a flat surface outside to measure rain or snowfall. Call your reports in to the TV station and watch the weather report for your information.

Related Jobs

Chemists and materials scientists, engineers, environmental scientists and specialists, geoscientists and hydrologists, mathematicians, physicists and astronomers

Education & Training
Bachelor's degree

Earnings
$$$$$

Job Outlook
Above-average increase

Chemists & Materials Scientists

On the Job

Chemists and materials scientists look for and use new information about chemicals and other materials. They create new paints, fibers, adhesives, drugs, and other products. They develop processes that save energy and reduce pollution. They make improvements in agriculture, medicine, and food processing. Most work in manufacturing firms or teach at universities.

Subjects to Study

Math, physics, chemistry, biology, computer science, business courses

Discover More

Have you ever mixed Mentos and diet soda? First stack a dozen Mentos candies on top of one another, using paper or an index card to keep them stacked together. Open a full 2-liter bottle of diet soda. Then drop the roll of candies all at once into the bottle and stand back. You might want to do this outdoors because the resulting eruption can get messy.

Related Jobs

Agricultural and food scientists, biological scientists, engineering and natural sciences managers, engineers, environmental scientists and specialists, geoscientists and hydrologists, medical scientists, physicists and astronomers, science technicians

Education & Training
Bachelor's degree

Earnings
$$$$$

Job Outlook
Little change

Environmental Scientists & Specialists

On the Job

Environmental scientists study the earth and humans' impact on it. Many are involved in the preservation of natural resources. All of these scientists play an important role in maintaining a healthy environment, designing waste-disposal sites, and cleaning up polluted land and water.

SOMETHING EXTRA

Population growth. Environmental degradation and restoration. Complex environmental laws. These reasons are why we'll need more environmental scientists and specialists. In addition, environmental scientists will be needed to help develop buildings, transportation corridors, and utilities that protect water and reflect good land use. Preventing environmental damage will provide many new opportunities for these workers.

Subjects to Study

Math, computer science, chemistry, physics, geology

Discover More

You don't have to have a college degree to begin thinking of ways to help the environment. Make a list of 10 things you can do—such as turning off lights when you leave the room or buying recycled paper—and share the list with your parents, friends, and teachers.

Related Jobs

Atmospheric scientists; biological scientists; chemists and materials scientists; conservation scientists and foresters; engineering technicians; engineers; geoscientists and hydrologists; physicists and astronomers; science technicians; surveyors, cartographers, photogrammetrists, and surveying and mapping technicians

Education & Training
Master's degree

Earnings
$$$$

Job Outlook
Rapid increase

Geoscientists & Hydrologists

On the Job

Geoscientists study the earth, focusing on its composition and geologic history. Many are involved in the search for natural resources while others concern themselves with cleaning up the environment. Oceanographers study the world's oceans and coastal waters. Hydrologists study the quantity and properties of water.

SOMETHING EXTRA

One of the hottest fields in geology is seismology—the study of earthquakes. And one of the biggest seismology experiments in history is still happening today in Parkfield, California. This small town is known for its regular pattern of earthquakes: For the last 150 years, Parkfield has experienced a magnitude 6 earthquake every 20 to 30 years. The latest struck in September 2004, finally giving researchers there something to write about.

Subjects to Study

Math, computer science, chemistry, physics, geology

Discover More

Earthquakes happen when tectonic plates of the earth's surface move. You can see the same effect by cracking the shell of a hard-boiled egg. The thin shell represents the earth's crust, moving around on the slippery mantle. Move the pieces of shell around. What happens when they collide? Eggquake!

Related Jobs

Atmospheric scientists; biological scientists; chemists and materials scientists; engineering technicians; engineers; environmental scientists and specialists; physicists and astronomers; science technicians; surveyors, cartographers, photogrammetrists, and surveying and mapping technicians

Education & Training
Master's degree

Earnings
$$$$$

Job Outlook
Above-average increase

Physicists & Astronomers

On the Job

Physicists study the matter that makes up the universe. They study forces of nature such as gravity, motion, and the nature of energy, electromagnetism, and nuclear interactions. They use their studies to design medical equipment, electronic devices, and lasers. Astronomers study the moon, sun, planets, galaxies, and stars. Their knowledge is used in space flight and navigation. Many teach in colleges and universities.

SOMETHING EXTRA

In the early 1940s, physicists working at a secret U.S. defense lab in Los Alamos, New Mexico, made a scientific breakthrough. They split an atom, setting off a chain of events that led directly to the atomic bombs dropped by the U.S. during World War II on Hiroshima and Nagasaki, Japan. Several of those scientists later regretted their work on the bomb. For better or worse, they assured their place in the history books and ushered in the atomic age.

Subjects to Study

Math, physics, chemistry, computer science, geology, astronomy

Discover More

One of the easiest ways to begin to learn more about astronomy is to become an amateur stargazer. Even without a telescope (though it certainly helps to have one, or at least a pair of binoculars), you can use a star chart to identify planets and constellations. Listen to the news for meteor showers and lunar eclipses.

Related Jobs

Atmospheric scientists, chemists and materials scientists, computer scientists, computer software engineers and computer programmers, engineering and natural sciences managers, engineers, environmental scientists and specialists, geoscientists and hydrologists, mathematicians, statisticians

Education & Training
Doctoral degree

Earnings
$$$$$

Job Outlook
Above-average increase

Economists

On the Job

Economists study how people use resources like land, labor, raw materials, and machinery to make products. They monitor inflation, interest rates, and employment levels. They use their studies to advise businesses and government agencies.

SOMETHING EXTRA

Interest is the extra fee that people pay for borrowing money from the bank. The amount of interest that people pay on loans for cars, houses, and credit cards changes from day to day. These interest rates are determined by the Federal Reserve Board and announced by its chairman. Because of this important power, even a whisper of activity by the Federal Reserve Board can cause the stock market to go up or down.

Subjects to Study

Math, English, economics, business courses, computer science, accounting

Discover More

Do you hear adults complain about the high cost of gasoline? Keep track of the price of premium gas at your local station each day over several weeks. Plot the price changes on a graph. Are the prices highest on certain days? On days when the prices are higher, do you think that news events caused the increase?

Related Jobs

Accountants and auditors; actuaries; budget analysts; cost estimators; financial analysts; financial managers; insurance underwriters; loan officers; management analysts; market and survey researchers; mathematicians; operations research analysts; personal financial advisors; purchasing managers, buyers, and purchasing agents; sociologists and political scientists; statisticians

Education & Training
Master's degree

Earnings
$$$$$

Job Outlook
Little change

Market & Survey Researchers

On the Job

Market and survey researchers tell businesses about the best ways to sell a product based on information they gather through interviews and questionnaires. Market research analysts might develop advertising brochures and commercials, sales plans, and product promotions such as rebates and giveaways. Some analysts are self-employed and must travel to work for different clients.

SOMETHING EXTRA

A market researcher might spend her day on the phone asking restaurants why they didn't buy more of a certain brand of crackers. Or she might invite groups of consumers to the office in the evening to test new products and give their opinions. Maybe you or your parents have been approached at the mall by someone with a clipboard wanting to ask your opinions. Market survey companies often have offices in malls because they can easily find lots of people to survey.

Subjects to Study

Economics, psychology, English, sociology, math, statistics

Discover More

Take a survey in your class. Buy several different kinds of tortilla chips. Then do a blind taste test. Blindfold several classmates and have them taste the chips. Keep a tally of which chips they prefer. Ask why they prefer one brand over another. These are the kinds of market surveys that researchers perform.

Related Jobs

Actuaries; advertising, marketing, promotions, public relations, and sales managers; cost estimators; economists; management analysts; mathematicians; operations research analysts; psychologists; public relations specialists; sociologists and political scientists; statisticians; urban and regional planners

Education & Training
Bachelor's degree

Earnings
$$$$

Job Outlook
Rapid increase

Psychologists

On the Job

Psychologists study the way people think, feel, and act. They work to understand, explain, and change people's behavior. They may conduct training programs, do market research, or provide counseling. They may work with mentally ill individuals. Psychologists work with schools, businesses, and health-care centers to help people deal with stress and changes in their lives, such as divorce and aging.

SOMETHING EXTRA

Psychologists sometimes use hypnosis to help people. They put a client into a deep trance and then make suggestions for changing a problem behavior. Although the person might not remember the suggestions when he or she is awake, they are planted deep in the subconscious and are triggered by the problem behavior. Hypnosis can be useful for people who want to quit smoking, lose weight, or overcome a fear.

Subjects to Study

English, psychology, statistics, communication skills, biology, physical sciences, computer science

Discover More

Try this experiment: Get a small fish in a bowl. Feed it at the same time every day. Each time you feed the fish, just before you put the food in the water, tap on the side of the bowl. Soon, when your fish sees you tap on the bowl, it will look for food on the water's surface. That's called conditioning!

Related Jobs

Audiologists; counselors; funeral directors; human resources, training, and labor relations managers and specialists; market and survey researchers; physicians and surgeons; recreation workers; social workers

Education & Training
Master's degree to Doctoral degree

Earnings
$$$$$

Job Outlook
Average increase

Urban & Regional Planners

On the Job

Urban and regional planners develop programs that encourage growth in communities and regions. They make plans for the best use of land and study the area's schools, hospitals, parks, roads, and other facilities to see whether they meet the needs of the community. They deal with legal codes and environmental issues, and a majority of them work for local governments. They often travel to inspect the features of the land to help in their planning.

SOMETHING EXTRA

Have you heard the term planned community? Whereas most cities simply grow as more people move in and open businesses, planned communities are plotted in detail before the first house is built. The Disney Corporation built a planned community in Florida that's made to look like an old-fashioned town. It's called Celebration, and it's an easy day's drive from Disney World (you know, in case you get bored at Disney World).

Subjects to Study

Math, English, speech, government, psychology, computer science, sociology, geography

Discover More

Plan a town on graph paper. Include all the roads, houses, schools, churches, and parks. Don't forget hospitals, police and fire stations, gas stations, sources for water and electricity, a shopping district, and a town center. A Starbucks is optional.

Related Jobs

Architects, except landscape and naval; civil engineers; landscape architects; environmental engineers; geographers; market and survey researchers; property, real estate, and community association managers; surveyors, cartographers, photogrammetrists, and surveying and mapping technicians

Education & Training
Master's degree

Earnings
$$$$

Job Outlook
Above-average increase

Sociologists & Political Scientists

On the Job

These workers study human society and political systems. Their research gives us insights into the ways that individuals, groups, and governments make decisions, use power, and respond to change. Through their studies, sociologists and political scientists suggest solutions to social, business, personal, and governmental problems.

Subjects to Study

Math, English, speech, government, psychology, computer science, sociology, history, political science, geography

Discover More

Do you have officers for your class or for a club? Were they elected? If so, why did they win? Write a paragraph analyzing the election.

Related Jobs

Archivists, curators, and museum technicians; counselors; economists; judges, magistrates, and other judicial workers; lawyers; market and survey researchers; news analysts, reporters, and correspondents; paralegals and legal assistants; psychologists; social scientists, other; social workers; statisticians; teachers—kindergarten, elementary, middle, and secondary; teachers—postsecondary; urban and regional planners

Education & Training
Master's degree

Earnings
$$$$$

Job Outlook
Rapid increase

Social Scientists, Other

On the Job

There are many kinds of social scientists. Anthropologists study the origins and development of human society, ancient ways of life, languages, tools, and archaeological remains. Geographers study how physical geography affects politics and culture. Historians research and interpret the past. Sociologists study social behavior and groups as well as religious, political, and business organizations.

> ### SOMETHING EXTRA
>
> Have you seen the Indiana Jones movies? How about The Mummy? Think that's what archaeology is all about? Think again! Most archaeologists spend years researching their subjects before beginning a major dig. Then months more are spent sifting through every artifact found, deciding what culture produced it and when. Of course, there are exciting moments. Imagine being the first human in 2,000 years to enter an ancient tomb and find gold. Just don't expect to dodge rolling boulders.

Subjects to Study

English, history, political science, sociology, mathematics, geography

Discover More

Imagine it is the year 3010 and anthropologists are studying humans from *our* day and age. How do you think they will describe us? What about our way of life, technology, culture, and beliefs will they find interesting, puzzling, or humorous? Write a couple of paragraphs analyzing our society from their point of view.

Related Jobs

Archivists, curators, and museum technicians; conservation scientists and foresters; counselors; economists; environmental scientists and specialists; geoscientists and hydrologists; market and survey researchers; psychologists; social workers

Education & Training
Master's degree

Earnings
$$$$

Job Outlook
Rapid increase

Science Technicians

On the Job

Science technicians use science and math to solve research problems. They investigate, invent, and help improve products. They set up, operate, and maintain lab equipment, monitor experiments, and record results. They may specialize in agriculture, biology, chemistry, or other sciences. Their work tends to be more practical. Some work outdoors and may be exposed to chemicals or radiation.

SOMETHING EXTRA

Finding new uses for agricultural crops can be important to areas that grow those crops. George Washington Carver's work is an excellent example of this. Carver, the son of slaves, developed hundreds of uses for two Southern crops: the peanut and the sweet potato. His work helped the South's economy and made him a nationally recognized scientist.

Subjects to Study

Math, physics, chemistry, biology, geology, shop and technology courses, computer science

Discover More

Science technicians need good eye-hand coordination and a good ability to follow written instructions. You can hone your skills by putting together model cars or model ships. Are the directions in the kit clear and easy to follow? How would you change them to make them clearer?

Education & Training
Associate degree to Bachelor's degree

Earnings
$$$

Related Jobs

Broadcast and sound engineering technicians and radio operators, clinical laboratory technologists and technicians, diagnostic medical sonographers, drafters, engineering technicians, radiologic technologists and technicians

Job Outlook
Average increase

Counselors

On the Job

Counselors help people with their problems; the work they do depends on the people they serve. School counselors help students with personal, social, and behavioral problems. College placement counselors help students decide on careers and find jobs. Rehabilitation counselors help people with disabilities and addictions. Employment counselors help people decide what kinds of jobs they want and help them find work.

SOMETHING EXTRA

Imagine losing everything in an earthquake or flood. You must find food, clothes, and a place to stay. You've lost your driver's license and credit cards, your car, maybe even family members or friends. The problems seem overwhelming. That's why counselors are brought in after disasters. They help victims obtain the basics—and talk about their grief or anger. That way, victims know they are not alone.

Subjects to Study

English, speech, psychology, social studies, sociology, computer skills, communication skills

Discover More

Talk to your school counselor about this job. What are the most difficult and most rewarding parts of the job? Find out what professional organizations he or she belongs to. Write to those organizations or visit their Web sites to learn more about counseling.

Related Jobs

Human resources, training, and labor relations managers and specialists; occupational therapists; physicians and surgeons; psychologists; registered nurses; social and human service assistants; social workers; teachers—kindergarten, elementary, middle, and secondary; teachers—special education

Education & Training
Bachelor's degree to Master's degree

Earnings
$$$

Job Outlook
Above-average increase

Health Educators

On the Job

Health educators teach people about healthy lifestyles and how to prevent disease, injury, and other problems. They discuss nutrition, exercise, and ways to avoid illness. They decide what information their audience needs and how to best meet those needs. Health educators work for colleges, schools, public health departments, nonprofit organizations, and private businesses.

SOMETHING EXTRA

Insurance companies, employers, and governments employ health educators to teach people how to live healthy lives and avoid costly treatments for illnesses. Some illnesses, such as lung cancer, heart disease, and skin cancer, may be avoided with lifestyle changes. Other illnesses are best treated with early detection, so it is important for people to learn how to detect problems on their own. Health educators help the public better understand the effects of behavior on health.

Subjects to Study

English, speech, psychology, biology, sociology, communication skills, health, nutrition, chemistry, anatomy, foreign languages

Discover More

Eating foods that are high in fat and sugar can cause health problems. Create a poster that explains this point and persuades people to eat food that is better for them.

Related Jobs

Counselors; psychologists; registered nurses; social and human service assistants; social workers; teachers—kindergarten, elementary, middle, and secondary

Education & Training
Bachelor's degree

Earnings
$$$

Job Outlook
Above-average increase

Probation Officers & Correctional Treatment Specialists

On the Job

Many people who are convicted of crimes are placed on probation instead of being sent to jail. Probation officers supervise these people, making sure they stay out of trouble. Correctional treatment specialists work with people in jails and prisons, evaluating their progress, planning special programs, and counseling offenders. All of these specialists work with criminal offenders, some of whom are dangerous.

SOMETHING EXTRA

What happens when a man commits a crime in Ohio but is captured in Florida? Or a woman is convicted in Utah but will serve her sentence in Illinois? Sometimes, prisoners are handcuffed and put on a regular airplane—with a guard, of course. But what about prisoners who are too dangerous for commercial flights? They have their own airline! The U.S. Marshals Service operates a fleet of planes to transport prisoners. Imagine how tight security must be on those flights!

Subjects to Study

English, speech, psychology, social studies, criminal justice, sociology

Discover More

Call your state's Department of Corrections, explain your interest in the job, and ask to interview a probation officer. What are the best parts of the job? What are the worst? Does the officer work from 9 to 5, or is he or she on call 24 hours a day? You can get more information on this job from the American Probation and Parole Association at www.appa-net.org.

Related Jobs

Correctional officers, counselors, firefighters, police and detectives, social and human service assistants, social workers

Education & Training
Bachelor's degree

Earnings
$$$$

Job Outlook
Above-average increase

Social & Human Service Assistants

On the Job

Social and human service assistants are in the business of helping people. They might work in a food bank, train mentally handicapped adults to do a job, or supervise groups of teenagers in a day program. They evaluate clients' needs, help them fill out the paperwork to get benefits, keep records, and file reports with social service agencies. They work in offices, hospitals, group homes, and private agencies.

Subjects to Study

English, speech, psychology, sociology, writing skills

Discover More

You can check out the social service field by volunteering at a food bank, an adult day-care center, or a community center in your neighborhood.

Related Jobs

Child care workers; correctional officers; counselors; eligibility interviewers, government programs; health educators; home health aides and personal and home care aides; occupational therapist assistants and aides; probation officers and correctional treatment specialists; psychologists; recreational therapists; social workers

Education & Training
Moderate-term OJT

Earnings
$$

Job Outlook
Rapid increase

Social Workers

On the Job

Social workers help people find solutions to their problems. They might help a client find housing, a job, or health care. They deal with issues like child abuse, poverty, unplanned pregnancy, alcohol or drug abuse, and criminal behavior. They help people cope with serious illnesses and crisis situations. They may work in hospitals, social service agencies, group homes, government agencies, or schools.

SOMETHING EXTRA

Do people tell you you're a good listener? Do you enjoy helping your friends figure out solutions to their problems? If so, social work might be a good field for you. A social worker's job is never the same from day to day. On Monday, you might help an elderly client find affordable housing, on Tuesday counsel a pregnant teenager, and on Wednesday visit a child in a foster home. Like many jobs in social service, the rewards often come from knowing you helped others.

Subjects to Study

English, communication skills, psychology, biology, sociology, history, foreign languages

Discover More

Talk to the counselor at your school about this job. Ask about the training and the kinds of situations he or she deals with on a daily basis. Ask whether he or she can help you set up a peer-counseling service at your school.

Related Jobs

Counselors, health educators, probation officers and correctional treatment specialists, psychologists, social and human service assistants

Education & Training
Bachelor's degree to Master's degree

Earnings
$$$

Job Outlook
Above-average increase

Court Reporters

On the Job

These workers put spoken words into writing. They make notes using shorthand or a stenotype machine, which prints shorthand. They also use audio recordings and computer voice translation software. They are often responsible for helping judges and attorneys access information. Sometimes they type as fast as 200 words per minute. Because they are the only ones recording what is being said, they must be accurate.

SOMETHING EXTRA

Have you noticed that many TV shows today are "closed captioned"? Closed captioning helps deaf people enjoy TV. Transcriptionists help create closed captioning. Using special equipment linked to computers, they type what is being said on the show. The words are printed at the bottom of the TV screen. You can see these captions if you press the mute button on your TV while watching a closed-captioned show.

Subjects to Study

English, word processing, spelling, foreign languages, computer skills, communication skills

Discover More

Watch an actual court case on TV. Find the court reporter in the courtroom and watch what he or she does. Listen to all the statements made by the lawyers, witnesses, and judge. Try to imagine correctly recording every word they say.

Related Jobs

Interpreters and translators, medical transcriptionists, paralegals and legal assistants, receptionists and information clerks, secretaries and administrative assistants

Education & Training
Voc/tech training

Earnings
$$$$

Job Outlook
Above-average increase

Judges, Magistrates & Other Judicial Workers

On the Job

Judges, magistrates, and other judicial workers oversee trials and make sure that everyone follows the court rules. They preside over all types of cases, from traffic tickets to murder trials. In court cases without a jury, the judge decides the verdict. All judges work for the government, either local, state, or federal. Nearly all judges have law degrees.

SOMETHING EXTRA

Not all judges wear black robes. In fact, judges at the state and federal levels are permitted to choose their attire. Though most of them go for the basic black, there are some exceptions. Former Chief Justice of the Supreme Court William Rehnquist had four gold bars on the sleeves of his gown, supposedly inspired by an opera he saw. And the seven judges of the Maryland Court of Appeals wear red robes instead of black. A formal dress code is still implicit, of course, so you won't find judges in tank tops and flip-flops.

Subjects to Study

English, writing skills, public speaking, government, history, foreign languages, psychology, computer science, criminal justice

Discover More

Have a mock trial in your social studies class. Different students can be lawyers for the prosecution and the defense, the defendant, the witnesses, the jury, and the judge. The judge has the final say about what evidence can and cannot be presented.

Related Jobs

Counselors, lawyers, paralegals and legal assistants, private detectives and investigators

Education & Training
Bachelor's degree +

Earnings
$$$$$

Job Outlook
Average increase

Lawyers

On the Job

Lawyers give people advice about the law and their rights. They represent people in court, presenting evidence that supports a client's position, asking questions, and arguing their case. Lawyers must do research to find the information they need to support their cases. They must have good reading, writing, and speaking skills. Lawyers may specialize in a number of areas, from corporate to criminal law.

SOMETHING EXTRA

Do you love to argue a point? Do you enjoy a good debate? Lawyers must be able to argue clearly and persuasively to convince the judge and jury of their points. But law isn't all about arguing. Lawyers spend hours researching their cases, questioning witnesses, looking for other cases that support their points, and studying the law. The brief flash in the courtroom is supported by lots of time in the library.

Subjects to Study

English, speech, government, history, foreign languages, psychology, computer skills, logic

Discover More

Organize a class debate. Pick a topic you feel strongly about, take a position, and argue your side. Be sure you do some research first—read articles and books on the topic and find out what other people think of it. Can you change your opponents' minds?

Related Jobs

Judges, magistrates, and other judicial workers; paralegals and legal assistants

Education & Training
Professional degree

Earnings
$$$$$

Job Outlook
Average increase

Paralegals & Legal Assistants

On the Job

Paralegals help lawyers prepare their cases. They do research and write reports that lawyers use to present their arguments in court. They may meet with clients to get information about a case, but they do not argue cases in court or set fees. Some paralegals have a wide variety of tasks, while others specialize in one area, such as tax law or publishing law.

SOMETHING EXTRA

Paralegals use computers to do their research. Special software packages and the Internet put a world of information at their fingertips. They simply enter a topic and receive a list of all documents on that subject. They also use computers to organize the volumes of paper needed to support cases. These programs help today's paralegals do in one day the work that used to take weeks.

Subjects to Study

English, business courses, computer skills, foreign languages, logic

Discover More

Contact a law firm or a legal-aid society in your area. Ask to talk to a paralegal. Find out what his or her duties involve. Ask how he or she became interested in the occupation and what kind of training the job requires. Also feel free to visit this Web site hosted by the National Association of Legal Assistants: www.nala.org.

Related Jobs

Claims adjusters, examiners, and investigators; occupational health and safety specialists; occupational health and safety technicians

Education & Training
Associate degree

Earnings
$$$$

Job Outlook
Rapid increase

Archivists, Curators & Museum Technicians

On the Job

These workers choose, buy, and care for collections of books, records, art, and other items for libraries and museums. The items might include coins, stamps, plants, paintings, sculptures, or even animals. They may work with records on paper, film, or computers. They plan exhibits, educational programs, and tours. Most work with the public and may travel to add to their collections.

SOMETHING EXTRA

Curators care about much more than Picasso or Michelangelo. The National Park Service, for example, operates hundreds of facilities, and many have museums and displays that are designed and maintained by curators. These curators might put together a wolf display at Yellowstone or a volcano display at Mount St. Helens. Or they might be in charge of the papers of Frederick Douglass or Jimmy Carter at their historic sites. It's a varied, exciting field.

Subjects to Study

English, speech, history, art, chemistry, physics, business courses, accounting

Discover More

Visit a museum or zoo in your area. Ask the tour guide about the collection. Who decides what to buy for the collection? Where do the exhibits come from? What would you like to see in the exhibit that's not already there?

Related Jobs

Artists and related workers; librarians; social scientists, other

Education & Training
Bachelor's degree to Master's degree

Earnings
$$$$

Job Outlook
Average increase

Instructional Coordinators

On the Job

Instructional coordinators develop teaching materials, train teachers, and assess school programs. They often specialize in a subject, such as language arts, math, or gifted and talented programs. Most work for school districts or independent consulting firms, and they spend time traveling between schools. The work can be stressful and involve long hours. Many instructional coordinators are former teachers and school administrators.

SOMETHING EXTRA

What happens when a school district's students aren't passing standardized tests? Most often, the district calls in a specialist to help research and solve the problem. As schools across the country place more emphasis on these tests, this job field is expected to grow rapidly. But keep in mind, the specialist is employed only as long as the district sees good results!

Subjects to Study

English, social sciences, business courses, psychology, computer science, foreign languages

Discover More

Call your school district's main offices and ask to interview the instructional coordinator or curriculum specialist. Does that person work only during the school year or year-round? What are the best and worst parts of the job?

Related Jobs

Counselors; education administrators; human resources, training, and labor relations managers and specialists; teachers—kindergarten, elementary, middle, and secondary; teachers—postsecondary; teachers—preschool, except special education; teachers—special education

Education & Training
Master's degree

Earnings
$$$$

Job Outlook
Rapid increase

Librarians

On the Job

Librarians help people use the library and its materials. They help people find the information they need and fill out applications for library cards. They may give talks on how to use the library or read to children during special programs. Some manage other workers, prepare budgets, and order materials. They may shelve books, update files, and design displays. They must be very computer literate and keep up with changes in technology.

SOMETHING EXTRA

The Royal Library of Alexandria was one of the oldest and largest libraries in history. Founded in Egypt in the third century B.C., it was believed to hold anywhere from 40,000 to 700,000 books. Housed in several buildings, it was thought to have been deliberately burned down, though by who remains a mystery. What also remains a mystery is how much those first librarians charged for overdue books.

Subjects to Study

English, literature, accounting, social sciences, business courses, psychology, computer science

Discover More

Take a tour of your school's library. Does your librarian order the books? How does he or she decide which books to order? What guidelines does your school district provide? Ask whether you can look through the publishers' catalogs and circle some titles that look interesting to you.

Related Jobs

Archivists, curators, and museum technicians; computer scientists; computer systems analysts; teachers—kindergarten, elementary, middle, secondary; teachers—postsecondary

Education & Training
Master's degree

Earnings
$$$$

Job Outlook
Average increase

Library Technicians & Library Assistants

On the Job

Library technicians and library assistants help librarians order, shelve, and organize materials. They help people find materials and information. They answer questions, help patrons check out materials, and may send notices for overdue books. They issue library cards and repair books. New technologies allow some of these workers to catalog new books. Library technicians and assistants may maintain the library's Web site and instruct patrons how to use the library's computers.

SOMETHING EXTRA

What happens when you want a book your library doesn't have? You can order it through the interlibrary loan system. This means that your library borrows the book from another library, usually one in your state, and then loans the book to you. Your librarian can search the records of other libraries, find the closest one that has the book you want, and key in an order. In just a few days, the book is in your hands!

Subjects to Study

English, literature, accounting, computer skills, business courses, math

Discover More

Check your local library for volunteer opportunities. You might be put to work shelving books, helping at the checkout counter, supervising small children during reading programs, or straightening up at the end of the day.

Related Jobs

Librarians, medical records and health information technicians, receptionists and information clerks, teacher assistants

Education & Training
Short-term OJT to Voc/tech training

Earnings
$$

Job Outlook
Average increase

Teacher Assistants

On the Job

Teacher assistants help children in the classroom and school cafeteria or on the playground and field trips. Sometimes they pay special attention to individual students or small groups who need more help with a subject. They help teachers by grading papers, keeping attendance records, filing, ordering supplies, helping out in the computer lab, or preparing class lessons.

Subjects to Study

English, communication skills, computer skills, math, foreign languages, speech, psychology

Discover More

Volunteer to help care for younger children at your school, church, or a local day-care center or youth organization. You might help them with schoolwork, play games, or teach a craft.

Related Jobs

Child care workers; library technicians and library assistants; occupational therapist assistants and aides; teachers—kindergarten, elementary, middle, and secondary; teachers—preschool, except special education; teachers—special education; teachers—vocational

Education & Training
Short-term OJT

Earnings
$

Job Outlook
Average increase

Teachers—Adult Literacy & Remedial Education

On the Job

Adult literacy and remedial education teachers teach basic skills courses—writing, reading, and math—to adults and out-of-school youths. They also work with people who want to update their job skills or prepare for the GED exam. An increasing number teach English as a second language to non-native speakers. Many work part-time, at night, or on the weekends.

SOMETHING EXTRA

Did you know that a significant portion of the adult population in the U.S. cannot read or struggles to read? Even people who graduate from high school sometimes have trouble reading. This makes it very hard to get and hold a job, to pay bills, or even to get a driver's license. Without reading skills, it's nearly impossible to get ahead in today's society.

Subjects to Study

English, communication and writing skills, math, social sciences, foreign languages

Discover More

Contact your local library about literacy programs they are running and ask whether they need volunteers. They may have you read stories to younger kids or become a reading tutor for someone learning the language.

Related Jobs

Counselors; interpreters and translators; social workers; teachers—kindergarten, elementary, middle, and secondary; teachers—postsecondary; teachers—preschool, except special education; teachers—special education; teachers, vocational

Education & Training
Bachelor's degree

Earnings
$$$$

Job Outlook
Above-average increase

Teachers—Postsecondary

On the Job

Postsecondary teachers work at colleges, community colleges, universities, and research facilities. They specialize in one field, such as history, physics, or journalism. They do research and write articles and books about their findings. Most professors hold advanced degrees. While many schools do not hold classes during the summer months, faculty still work year-round, preparing lectures, attending seminars, and conducting research.

Subjects to Study

English, math, speech, sciences, social sciences, foreign languages, computer science

Discover More

Visit a college campus and sit in on a class or two. Watch the professor and think about how the class resembles or differs from your classes at school. Talk to the professor after class and ask about the job.

Related Jobs

Authors, writers, and editors; counselors; education administrators; librarians; management analysts; public relations specialists; teachers—kindergarten, elementary, middle, and secondary; teachers—vocational

Education & Training
Professional degree

Earnings
$$$$

Job Outlook
Above-average increase

Teachers—Preschool, Except Special Education

On the Job

Preschool teachers nurture, teach, and care for children usually aged 3 to 5. These teachers plan and implement a curriculum that covers areas of a child's development, such as motor skills, social and emotional development, and language development. They introduce children to reading and writing, arts, science, and social studies. These teachers use games, music, art, books, computers, and other tools to teach concepts and skills.

SOMETHING EXTRA

Children love to play, so preschool teachers use fun methods to develop their students' language and vocabulary, improve social skills, and introduce science and math concepts. For example, storytelling, rhyming games, and acting games can help children's language use. Having children work together to build a neighborhood in a sandbox develops their social abilities. Showing children how to balance blocks when building a bridge uses science and math.

Subjects to Study

English, communication skills, child development, family and consumer sciences, art, music, drama, health, speech, psychology

Discover More

Invent a new way to teach preschool children how to count from 1 to 10. Use a game, music, art, or drama to make it fun!

Related Jobs

Child care workers; teacher assistants; teachers—kindergarten, elementary, middle, secondary; teachers—special education

Education & Training
Voc/tech training

Earnings
$

Job Outlook
Above-average increase

Teachers—Kindergarten, Elementary, Middle & Secondary

On the Job

Teachers help students learn in school. They plan lessons, prepare tests, grade papers, and write reports of students' progress. They meet with parents and school staff to talk about grades and problems. Some teach a specific grade; others teach one subject to students in many grades. Most work more than 40 hours a week, and some work second jobs during the summer months. Many supervise school activities such as clubs and sports teams.

SOMETHING EXTRA

Think about the challenges of being a working parent. You have to find someone to watch your kids while you are at work. This is hard enough during the school year, but in the summers and on winter break, it's especially tough. One of the things many teachers like about teaching is that they get the same days off as their kids. This cuts down on child-care costs and lets them plan vacations and activities for the whole family.

Subjects to Study

English, social studies, math, sciences, psychology, foreign languages, computer science

Discover More

Talk with your school counselor about programs such as peer tutoring or cadet teaching in your school. You can help younger students who are having trouble with a subject or grade papers for a teacher.

Related Jobs

Athletes, coaches, umpires, and related workers; child care workers; counselors; education administrators; librarians; social workers; teacher assistants; teachers—postsecondary; teachers—preschool, except special education; teachers—special education; teachers—vocational

Education & Training
Bachelor's degree

Earnings
$$$$

Job Outlook
Average increase

Teachers—Self-Enrichment Education

On the Job

Self-enrichment teachers usually know a lot about a certain subject and are willing to share what they know with students (mostly adults) who are eager to learn. They may teach classes in cooking, literature, art, financial planning, spirituality, or any number of other topics. Most self-enrichment classes are informal and are designed for individuals who want to improve themselves, enrich their lives, or learn more about a topic.

SOMETHING EXTRA

Woodworking, Tai Chi, cooking, hiking, ballroom dancing—these are some of the classes offered through enrichment education programs. People take these courses because they are fun and interesting. Whether it's discussing romance novels or teaching someone how to use a digital camera, you can be sure everyone in the class wants to be there and enjoys learning about the subject.

Subjects to Study

English, social studies, social sciences, computer science, art, dance, physical education

Discover More

Call a local community college or high school and ask for the catalog of continuing-education courses. Find a class that interests you, then call the school and ask whether you can sit in on a session of that class.

Related Jobs

Artists and related workers; athletes, coaches, umpires, and related workers; dancers and choreographers; musicians, singers, and related workers; recreation workers; teachers—kindergarten, elementary, middle, and secondary; teachers—preschool, except special education

Education & Training
Work experience

Earnings
$$$

Job Outlook
Rapid increase

Teachers—Special Education

On the Job

Special education teachers work with students who have disabilities. Most work in elementary, middle, or high schools, but some work with toddlers and preschoolers. They prepare classes to meet their students' needs, grade papers, and write reports. They may teach academic studies or life skills. They help to come up with the best school plan for each student.

SOMETHING EXTRA

Say "special education" and many people think of classrooms for learning-disabled students. But that's only part of the picture. Special education covers classes for students with mental disabilities, physical disabilities, and emotional problems. It includes classes for gifted and talented students. Special education classes spread from preschool and early-intervention programs to continued classes for adults with disabilities. It's a wide and growing field.

Subjects to Study

English, social studies, math, sciences, psychology, computer science, art, dance, physical education

Discover More

Arrange with your teacher to spend a day observing a special education class at your school. Watch how the teacher interacts with the students. You might be able to help by reading to younger children or tutoring them.

Related Jobs

Audiologists; counselors; occupational therapists; psychologists; recreational therapists; social workers; speech-language pathologists; teacher assistants; teachers—kindergarten, elementary, middle, and secondary; teachers—preschool, except special education; teachers—vocational

Education & Training
Bachelor's degree

Earnings
$$$$

Job Outlook
Above-average increase

Teachers—Vocational

On the Job

Vocational education teachers, commonly called *career and technical education (CTE) teachers* or *career-technology teachers*, train students to work in a wide variety of fields. These fields include agricultural science, family and consumer science, health care, business and marketing, trade and industry, and technology. Vocational education teachers give students practical skills in occupations. They may work with students at special career schools and in school shops and labs.

Subjects to Study

English, math, social studies, sciences, psychology, computer science, shop, family and consumer science

Discover More

Learn about the kind of vocational programs offered by high schools in your area. To accomplish this task, talk to your school counselor and research the high school programs online. How many different kinds of programs did you discover? Did anything about these programs surprise you? Do any of the programs interest you? Why or why not?

Education & Training
Bachelor's degree +

Earnings
$$$$

Related Jobs

Counselors; education administrators; librarians; teachers—kindergarten, elementary, middle, and secondary school; teachers—preschool, except special education; teachers—special education

Job Outlook
Average increase

Artists & Related Workers

On the Job

Artists use a variety of methods and materials to communicate through art. They might use oil paints, watercolors, pencils, clay, chalk, or even scrap metal to create their work. Visual artists are usually called graphic artists or fine artists. Graphic artists use art to meet the needs of business clients, such as stores, ad agencies, and service providers. Fine artists create artwork to sell and display in museums or galleries. More than half are self-employed and must use good business skills to be successful.

SOMETHING EXTRA

When she was in her late 70s, a time when most other people have retired or are retiring, Grandma Moses decided to try her hand at a completely new job: She became an artist. This famous American painter recorded scenes of life on the farm. Her style, which resembles the way a child might paint, is known as primitivism.

Subjects to Study

Art, drawing, drafting, computer skills, English, business courses

Discover More

The best way to prepare for this career is to take art classes, visit museums, study the styles of other artists, and practice, practice, practice.

Related Jobs

Archivists, curators, and museum technicians; commercial and industrial designers; computer programmers; computer software engineers and desktop publishers; fashion designers; graphic designers; jewelers and precious stone and metal workers; photographers; woodworkers

Education & Training
Long-term OJT to
Bachelor's degree +

Earnings
$$$$

Job Outlook
Average increase

Commercial & Industrial Designers

On the Job

These individuals are responsible for the look, feel, function, quality, and safety of most of the products we use every day. They combine knowledge of art, engineering, and business to create sketches and models that are then used in production. Often commercial and industrial designers specialize in one product, from automobiles to furniture. They are sometimes involved in testing and marketing products, and many of them are self-employed.

> ## SOMETHING EXTRA
>
> One of the more famous stories of industrial design concerns Post-it Notes—those little colored pieces of paper you see all over desks and offices. A researcher at 3M set out to make a stronger adhesive but ultimately developed a weaker one that just barely stuck. Three years later, a fellow researcher at the company discovered he could coat scraps of paper with the stuff and use them as bookmarks. They would stick, but could be lifted off with ease. Now they are everywhere.

Subjects to Study

Art, drawing, drafting, business courses, English, computer skills

Discover More

On paper, design a brand-new hybrid car or sports car. Be sure to design both the exterior and the interior. Will it have fold-down seats? A navigation system? Where will people put their cups? Don't forget the safety features. Check out car magazines and Web sites for ideas.

Related Jobs

Architects, except landscape and naval; artists and related workers; computer software engineers and computer programmers; desktop publishers; drafters; engineers; fashion designers; floral designers; graphic designers; interior designers

Education & Training
Bachelor's degree

Earnings
$$$$

Job Outlook
Average increase

Fashion Designers

On the Job

Fashion designers create the clothing, shoes, and accessories worn by billions of people. They research fashion trends, sketch designs, select materials, create prototypes, and oversee the production of their items. Some design costumes for movies, television, and plays. Well over half of all fashion designers work in either California or New York.

Subjects to Study

Family and consumer sciences, art, drawing, business courses, English, computer skills

Discover More

Talk to your teacher and principal about having a fall or spring fashion show. Head a committee to help with the planning, including choosing styles, models, and music. Charge a small entrance fee and give the proceeds to a local charity.

Related Jobs

Artists and related workers; commercial and industrial designers; floral designers; graphic designers; interior designers; jewelers and precious stone and metal workers; models; textile, apparel, and furnishings occupations

Education & Training
Associate degree

Earnings
$$$$

Job Outlook
Little change

Floral Designers

On the Job

Floral designers select flowers, greenery, ribbons, and containers and produce arrangements for decoration and special occasions. Most work independently or in small shops doing designs for special events like weddings and funerals. Others work in the wholesale floral business or in the floral departments in grocery stores. Floral designers often work under deadlines (the flowers need to be fresh, after all).

SOMETHING EXTRA

The average cost for flowers at a wedding ranges from $500 to $1,500. If that sounds like a lot, it helps to put it into context: The average total bill for a wedding is $22,000. The good news for floral designers is that people will continue to get married despite the cost, so there will always be a market for their services.

Subjects to Study

Botany, biology, family and consumer sciences, art, business courses, English

Discover More

If you have a flower garden at home, ask your parents whether you can pick a selection of them and make a table arrangement (be sure to ask for a vase as well). Alternatively, go to the grocery store and select a bouquet with a variety of flowers. Take it home and separate each stem. Then make your own original arrangement.

Related Jobs

Artists and related workers, commercial and industrial designers, fashion designers, graphic designers, interior designers, landscape architects

Education & Training
Short-term OJT

Earnings
$

Job Outlook
Declining

Graphic Designers

On the Job

Otherwise known as graphic artists, these designers decide the best way to communicate a message in print, film, or electronic format. Some graphic designers develop the layout of Web sites, newspapers, and magazines, while others work in advertising on packaging and marketing materials. Graphic designers are expected to be familiar with the latest computer design software.

Subjects to Study

Art, drawing, drafting, business courses, English, computer skills

Discover More

On paper, create a new logo for your school. You might want to create a new mascot and motto as well. Consider how the logo might appeal to parents, students, and teachers alike. What colors look best together? What overall message do you want the new logo to send?

Related Jobs

Advertising, marketing, promotions, public relations, and sales managers; artists and related workers; authors, writers, and editors; commercial and industrial designers; computer software engineers and computer programmers; desktop publishers; drafters; fashion designers; floral designers; interior designers; photographers; prepress technicians and workers

Education & Training
Bachelor's degree

Earnings
$$$

Job Outlook
Average increase

Interior Designers

On the Job

Interior designers are responsible for designing and arranging the physical space within a building, whether it's a home, hospital, theater, restaurant, or office. They experiment with colors, textures, furniture, lighting, and space to create a safe, functional, and pleasing atmosphere. More and more often they are involved in planning the layouts of buildings as well.

SOMETHING EXTRA

Perhaps you have heard of Feng Shui. This ancient Chinese practice stems from Taoism and is concerned with achieving harmony with your surroundings. Through a careful arrangement of space, it is believed you can increase the flow of positive energy. Though originally based on a combination of philosophy and scientific calculation, it has been viewed as both a fad and a superstition in the United States.

Subjects to Study

Art, business courses, English, computer skills, family and consumer sciences, shop courses

Discover More

On paper, redesign a room of your home. Check out magazines for ideas. Get paint and wallpaper samples from the hardware store. Will you recover the furniture in new fabric? Hang new drapes? Replace the flooring? Decide on a color scheme and draw the room.

Related Jobs

Architects, except landscape and naval; artists and related workers; commercial and industrial designers; fashion designers; floral designers; graphic designers; landscape architects

Education & Training
Associate degree

Earnings
$$$

Job Outlook
Above-average increase

Actors, Producers & Directors

On the Job

Actors, producers, and directors make words come alive through plays, TV shows, and films. Actors play characters, speaking the lines written in the script and adding their own movements. Directors choose plays and scripts, select the actors, and conduct rehearsals for productions. Producers arrange the financing and decide the size of the production and the budget. Directors and producers often work under tight deadlines and stressful conditions.

SOMETHING EXTRA

Making it as an actor is tough. That's why most actors work at least part-time at another job while they wait for their big break. For example, Brad Pitt donned a chicken suit for a fast-food restaurant in California. Steve Carell delivered mail. And comedienne Whoopi Goldberg worked as a funeral parlor cosmetician, observing, "I'd rather work on dead people. They don't move."

Subjects to Study

English, speech, drama, music, dance, art, photography, business courses

Discover More

You can learn more about the theater by auditioning for a role in a school or community play. If being on stage is not for you, try working backstage, making props, working the lights or sound system, or helping with costumes and makeup.

Related Jobs

Announcers; dancers and choreographers; fashion designers; musicians, singers, and related workers; top executives

Education & Training
Long-term OJT to Bachelor's degree +

Earnings
$$$$

Job Outlook
Average increase

Athletes, Coaches, Umpires & Related Workers

On the Job

From football to ice skating, professional athletes train every day to stay in top physical condition for competition. Coaches organize, lead, teach, and referee indoor and outdoor games such as volleyball and soccer. Some also teach specific skills, such as weight training, tennis, and gymnastics. Umpires make sure everyone follows the rules and sometimes have to make tough decisions. All of these jobs are very competitive.

SOMETHING EXTRA

Do you have what it takes to be a professional athlete? The answer, sadly, is probably not. Here are the facts: Every year in America, more than 1 million young men play high school football; another 500,000 play basketball and baseball. How many make it to the pros? To put it in perspective, consider this: Only about 2 out of every 10,000 high school athletes sign a professional sports contract. Here's another sobering statistic: The average professional sports career lasts just four years.

Subjects to Study

Physical education, nutrition, biology, anatomy, sports education

Discover More

Participate in sports or physical-fitness activities at your school or local gym or YMCA. Take classes in an activity that interests you, then ask whether you can be a team member, team manager, or coach's assistant.

Related Jobs

Dietitians and nutritionists; fitness workers; physical therapists; recreational therapists; recreation workers; teachers—kindergarten, elementary, middle, and secondary

Education & Training
Long-term OJT

Earnings
$$

Job Outlook
Rapid increase

Dancers & Choreographers

On the Job

Dancers express ideas and stories through the movement of their bodies. Dance styles include classical ballet, modern dance, tap, jazz, and different folk dances. Dancers perform in musicals, operas, TV shows, movies, music videos, and commercials. Dancers must be strong, coordinated, and dedicated. Choreographers create dances and teach dancers. They may work for one company or on a freelance basis. Those who operate their own studios must have good business skills.

SOMETHING EXTRA

Pointe ballet training traditionally starts at the age of 12, although regular ballet classes usually start much earlier. Most dancers have their first professional auditions by the time they are 17 or 18. But the training and practice for professional ballet dancers never ends. Most professional dancers work out for several hours every day. By the time they are 30, most are done with their performing days and move into teaching and choreography.

Subjects to Study

Music, dance, physical education, drama, English, history

Discover More

Sign up for dance classes at a local studio. Try several styles, from ballet to tap to swing. Ask the teacher about the job. Does he or she work at another job in addition to teaching? Does he or she perform with a dance company? Be sure to attend dance performances as well.

Related Jobs

Actors, producers, and directors; athletes, coaches, umpires, and related workers; fashion designers; musicians, singers, and related workers; set and exhibit designers

Education & Training
Long-term OJT to Work experience

Earnings
$$$

Job Outlook
Little change

Musicians, Singers & Related Workers

On the Job

Musicians and singers play instruments and perform vocal music. They may perform alone or in groups, before live audiences or in recording studios. Composers write original songs for bands, orchestras, or singers. Conductors lead musical groups such as orchestras, dance bands, and ensembles. Most musicians work nights and weekends and must travel to perform. Because it's so hard to support themselves with music, many take other jobs as well. Many musicians work in cities with recording studios, such as New York, Los Angeles, and Nashville.

> ## SOMETHING EXTRA
>
> Did you ever wonder what famous musicians did before they were famous? Some, like Taylor Swift, hit it big early, but others had to work their way up from obscurity. Garth Brooks, for instance, beefed up as a nightclub bouncer while waiting to be discovered. Mariah Carey worked nights as a janitor in a beauty salon. As for Madonna—the ultimate material girl—she did counter duty at the Times Square Dunkin' Donuts.

Subjects to Study

Vocal music, instrumental music, English, creative writing, business courses

Discover More

Participate in your school band, orchestra, or choir. Audition for a role in a school or community musical. Take lessons to learn a musical instrument.

Related Jobs

Actors, producers, and directors; announcers; dancers and choreographers

Education & Training
Long-term OJT to Bachelor's degree

Earnings
$$$

Job Outlook
Average increase

Announcers

On the Job

Radio announcers (or disc jockeys) plan and perform radio programs. They may choose and play music, interview guests, and write program material. Television announcers and newscasters prepare and present the news, weather, and sports, although most specialize in one of these areas. They may work unusual hours, including very early in the morning and very late at night. When emergency situations arise, they must be there to cover them for the news.

SOMETHING EXTRA

What did people do to entertain themselves before television? Well, in the 1940s and earlier, families gathered around the radio after dinner and listened to mysteries, comedies, Westerns, variety shows, and even soap operas. Radio stars in those days were as popular as today's TV stars—without all of the makeup or the tabloids, of course.

Subjects to Study

English, public speaking, drama, foreign languages, electronics, computers

Discover More

Ask the principal at your school if you can make the morning announcements one day. Write out your "intro" and try to make it humorous or catchy. Can you entertain your audience members while you keep them informed? That's the job of an announcer.

Related Jobs

Actors, producers, and directors; authors, writers, and editors; broadcast and sound engineering technicians and radio operators; interpreters and translators; musicians, singers, and related workers; news analysts, reporters, and correspondents; public relations specialists

Education & Training
Moderate-term OJT to Long-term OJT

Earnings
$$

Job Outlook
Declining

Authors, Writers & Editors

On the Job

Authors and writers write novels and nonfiction books, articles, scripts, plays, poems, and ads. They must also be able to sell what they have written. Editors choose the stories and books that publishing houses will print or post online. Magazine editors choose articles for publication and assign stories to writers. Many of them also write stories and articles. Editors also review, rewrite, and correct the work of writers.

SOMETHING EXTRA

So you want to be a writer, but you can't find time to write? Next time you feel that way, consider Anthony Trollope. This English novelist in the 1800s worked full time at the post office, yet managed to write dozens of books that are still in print. How did he find the time? He wrote by the clock—producing a set number of pages every day. Trollope once wrote, "Three hours a day will produce as much as a man ought to write." So unless you have two full-time jobs, there should be nothing stopping you.

Subjects to Study

English, creative writing, journalism, computer skills, history, psychology

Discover More

Submit a story to a local newspaper or magazine. Check out *The Writer's Market* for those publications, such as *Stone Soup,* that encourage young writers. You could also enter a writing contest.

Related Jobs

Announcers; interpreters and translators; news analysts, reporters, and correspondents; technical writers

Education & Training
Short-term OJT to Bachelor's degree

Earnings
$$$$

Job Outlook
Average increase

Broadcast & Sound Engineering Technicians & Radio Operators

On the Job

Broadcast and sound engineering technicians work with electronic equipment to record and transmit radio and television programs. They operate, install, and repair microphones, TV cameras, recorders, and antennas. They often work holidays, weekends, and evenings for news programs. When disasters happen, they must be on the scene to record the news. Setting up equipment sometimes requires heavy lifting and climbing.

SOMETHING EXTRA

Did you ever wonder how a moviemaker got a certain sound—maybe the hum of a spacecraft engine or the blast of a star exploding? The soundtrack in a movie is made by sound mixers, using everything from explosives to cabbage to corn flakes. Using a process called dubbing, sound mixers sit at a console facing the movie screen and add the special-effect sounds and music. The sounds are then mixed on one master, which becomes the movie's soundtrack.

Subjects to Study

Math, shop courses, physics, electronics, English, computer skills

Discover More

Build your own electronic equipment using a hobby kit. Check a toy or hobby store to see what kind of equipment is available. Operating a "ham" or amateur radio is great experience for this occupation.

Related Jobs

Communications equipment operators, computer support specialists, electrical and electronics installers and repairers, engineering technicians, science technicians

Education & Training
Short-term OJT to Associate degree

Earnings
$$$

Job Outlook
Average increase

Young Person's Occupational Outlook Handbook, © JIST Works

Interpreters & Translators

On the Job

Interpreters and translators convert spoken and written words from one language into another. These language specialists also relay concepts and ideas between languages. They must thoroughly understand the subject about which they are translating. They also need to be sensitive to other cultures. This work can be sporadic, and many interpreters and translators work part time.

SOMETHING EXTRA

Did you know that one out of every five Americans speaks a language other than English at home? That's more than 50 million people who speak Spanish, Chinese, French, German, Russian, or some other language. So imagine the growing need for people who can translate and interpret between English and these languages. Many businesses and government agencies have an urgent need for translators to help them communicate with their customers.

Subjects to Study

English, speech, foreign languages, computer skills

Discover More

The United Nations is an assembly of representatives from countries all over the world. The UN's job is to maintain international peace and security, to develop friendly relations among nations, to help solve international problems, and to promote human rights and freedoms. Its headquarters in New York employs many translators. Learn more about the UN at www. un.org/Pubs/CyberSchoolBus.

Education & Training
Long-term OJT

Earnings
$$$

Related Jobs

Authors, writers and editors; court reporters; medical transcriptionists; teachers—adult literacy and remedial education; teachers—kindergarten, elementary, middle, and secondary; teachers—postsecondary

Job Outlook
Rapid increase

News Analysts, Reporters & Correspondents

On the Job

News analysts, reporters, and correspondents gather information and write articles or deliver reports about events around the world. Some take photographs or shoot videos. Radio and television reporters often report live from the scene of a crime or disaster. The work is usually hectic and stressful, and the deadlines are tight. Reporting can be dangerous work and requires long hours, irregular schedules, and lots of travel.

SOMETHING EXTRA

Though it might seem glamorous to be in front of the camera, reporters and correspondents are often called upon to do dangerous work. Though every precaution is taken to ensure their safety, war correspondents often find themselves in potentially deadly situations. The war in Iraq, begun in March 2003, had claimed the lives of 140 journalists six years later, nearly double the number of journalists as were killed in the Vietnam conflict.

Subjects to Study

English, journalism, social studies, history, creative writing, speech, computer skills, foreign languages

Discover More

Collect three or more newspapers that are all reporting on the same story. Read the reports and then make notes about how each newspaper's story differs from the others. The facts may be the same, but one paper may choose to play up sensational aspects while another pushes a different viewpoint.

Education & Training
Bachelor's degree

Earnings
$$$

Related Jobs

Announcers, interpreters and translators; authors, writers, and editors; public relations specialists

Job Outlook
Declining

Photographers

On the Job

Photographers use cameras to record people, places, and events. Most of these workers specialize in commercial, portrait, or journalistic photography. Commercial photographers may take school or wedding pictures or photos for ads. Portrait photographers work in studios, taking pictures of people for special occasions. Journalistic photographers work for newspapers and magazines.

SOMETHING EXTRA

Photojournalists use their cameras to record history and news events for magazines and newspapers. It can be dangerous work. In 1992, Dan Eldon, a photographer from the Philadelphia Inquirer, went to Somalia to document the famine there. Because of his work, the U.S. began delivering food supplies to the war-ravaged country—a move that was not popular with some of the Somalian leaders. Less than a year later, Eldon was stoned to death by a mob in Somalia. He was 22 years old.

Subjects to Study

English, journalism, photography, art, creative writing, business courses, computer skills

Discover More

Take photos of special people and places in your life. Try using different kinds of settings. For example, turn off the flash when you might normally use it. Zoom in to take pictures of small flowers and insects. Create a digital album of your best work and send it to friends or post it online.

Related Jobs

Artists and related workers; commercial and industrial designers; desktop publishers; graphic designers; news analysts, reporters, and correspondents; prepress technicians and workers; television, video, and motion picture camera operators and editors

Education & Training
Long-term OJT

Earnings
$$

Job Outlook
Average increase

Public Relations Specialists

On the Job

Public relations specialists work to present a good image of their clients to the public. Their job is to make sure the clients' good news is spread far and wide and to put a positive spin on bad news. They write press releases and speeches and set up "photo opportunities" of their clients doing good things. Many work more than 40 hours a week. In an emergency, they may be on call around the clock.

Subjects to Study

English, creative writing, journalism, psychology, sociology, computer skills, speech, foreign languages

Discover More

Write a weekly press release for your class, announcing some good news or interesting event. Be sure the release is honest but puts forth the best possible image. Keep it short and snappy to be sure it gets attention!

Related Jobs

Advertising, marketing, promotions, public relations, and sales managers; demonstrators and product promoters; lawyers; market and survey researchers; news analysts, reporters, and correspondents; sales representatives, wholesale and manufacturing

Education & Training
Bachelor's degree

Earnings
$$$$

Job Outlook
Rapid increase

Technical Writers

On the Job

These workers write training and operating manuals, online help, assembly instructions, computer program documentation, and users' guides. They specialize in making technical information easy to understand. They work in engineering, science, electronics, information technology, health care, and other complex areas. New discoveries and developments are creating demand for writers who can interpret technical facts for a general audience. Some technical writers work on a freelance or contract basis.

SOMETHING EXTRA

Businesses, organizations, and governments are making more material available online in various formats. Customers and the public can now access and share the information easily and scrutinize it closely. Technical writers must revise and update online content quickly to fix errors, clarify facts, address new situations, and keep all details current. This trend will continue as the amount and complexity of information on the Web grows.

Subjects to Study

English, writing, journalism, computer skills, math

Discover More

Ask a family member for the instructions that came with an electronic device, such as a smart phone, computer, or television. Read the instructions. Do you understand them? Is the information in a step-by-step or other format that makes it easy to follow? What questions do you have after reading the instructions? Do you see a way to improve them?

Related Jobs

Announcers; authors, writers, and editors; interpreters and translators; public relations specialists

Education & Training
Bachelor's degree

Earnings
$$$$

Job Outlook
Above-average increase

Television, Video & Motion Picture Camera Operators & Editors

On the Job

Camera operators work behind the scenes on TV shows, documentaries, motion pictures, and industrial films. They shoot the film you see on-screen, sometimes from high up on scaffolding or flat on their bellies on the ground. They may work long, irregular hours all over the world. Film editors look at the hundreds of hours of film for a project and decide which scenes to include and which to cut to produce the final product.

SOMETHING EXTRA

For a good view of what's possible in filmmaking, rent the movie *Forrest Gump*. Among other tricks, the filmmakers spliced and altered vintage film to show the hero shaking hands with John F. Kennedy, more than 30 years after Kennedy's death. Or take the case of the character Gollum from the *Lord of the Rings* movies, a character created through CGI (computer-generated imagery). Rapid changes in technology make this an exciting and demanding profession.

Subjects to Study

English, journalism, photography, art, business courses, electronics

Discover More

Use a digital camcorder to make your own movie. These cameras let you load your movie onto a computer and then alter the images in countless ways. Give your leading lady green hair, edit in an explosion or two, drop in a few aliens, and make your own science-fiction flick.

Related Jobs

Artists and related workers, broadcast and sound engineering technicians and radio operators, graphic designers, photographers

Education & Training
Bachelor's degree

Earnings
$$$$

Job Outlook
Average increase

Audiologists

On the Job

Audiologists work with people who cannot hear as well as they should. They use audiometers, computers, and other testing devices to diagnose hearing and balance disorders. They recommend treatments such as hearing aids, implants, or surgery. They work in hospitals, nursing homes, and schools. Those who work in private practice must have good business sense.

SOMETHING EXTRA

Heather Whitestone McCallum, Miss America 1995, was deaf most of her life until doctors restored her hearing in 2002. She communicated through speaking and dancing and lived quite successfully in a hearing world. Deaf actress Marlee Matlin won an Academy Award for her role in the movie *Children of a Lesser God* and has had several TV roles, including a stint on *Seinfeld* and a recurring role as a political aide on *The West Wing*.

Subjects to Study

English, math, physics, chemistry, biology, psychology

Discover More

You have probably had a hearing test at school. The next time hearing tests are being done at your school, ask the nurse or other person giving the test to tell you more about it. How does it measure hearing loss? What happens if a student is found to have a hearing loss?

Related Jobs

Occupational therapists, optometrists, physical therapists, psychologists, speech-language pathologists

Education & Training
Professional degree

Earnings
$$$$

Job Outlook
Rapid increase

Chiropractors

On the Job

Chiropractors help people who have problems with their muscles, nerves, or skeleton, especially the spine. They examine patients, order tests, and take X-rays. They treat patients by massaging or adjusting the spinal column. They use water and heat therapy. They stress nutrition, exercise, and reducing stress in treatment. They do not prescribe drugs or perform surgery. Many are self-employed.

SOMETHING EXTRA

What does a chiropractor have to do with treating headaches? As it turns out, quite a lot. Headaches can result from poor posture, tension, or a misalignment of the spinal cord. Using massage, heat therapy, and realignment exercises and techniques, chiropractors can help people who suffer from persistent or chronic headaches. They teach people how to prevent headaches in the first place, which might be the best treatment of all.

Subjects to Study

Health, biology, anatomy, nutrition, chemistry, physics, psychology, math

Discover More

Aromatherapy is the practice of using different smells to relax, calm, or energize yourself. Try an experiment at home. Buy several different scented candles. Each evening at dinner, light a different candle. (Get your parents' permission first!) How do the different scents affect your mood (or your appetite)?

Education & Training
Professional degree

Earnings
$$$$$

Related Jobs

Athletic trainers, massage therapists, occupational therapists, physical therapists, physicians and surgeons, podiatrists, veterinarians

Job Outlook
Above-average increase

Dentists

On the Job

Dentists help people take care of their teeth. They remove teeth and straighten them with braces, repair broken teeth, and fill cavities. They may replace a patient's original teeth with a "bridge" of false teeth. They may also perform surgery to treat gum disease. They teach people how to brush, floss, and care for their teeth to prevent problems. They wear masks, gloves, and safety glasses to protect themselves from infectious diseases. Many are self-employed.

SOMETHING EXTRA

Dentists have been practicing for nearly 7,000 years, although you might not recognize some of the treatments used back then as dentistry. In ancient Babylon, for example, "dentists" used worms, prayers, and herbs to treat tooth decay. In the Middle Ages, dentists were considered the first surgeons—although about all they could do was remove teeth, which they did to treat nearly every condition you can think of.

Subjects to Study

Biology, anatomy, chemistry, physics, health, math, business courses

Discover More

The next time you visit your dentist—and before you have to open wide—ask him or her about the job. What kind of training is available in your area? What is the best part of the job? What's the worst? Is your dentist bothered that so many people are afraid of dentists?

Related Jobs

Chiropractors, optometrists, physicians and surgeons, podiatrists, veterinarians

Education & Training
Professional degree

Earnings
$$$$$

Job Outlook
Above-average increase

Dietitians & Nutritionists

On the Job

Dietitians and nutritionists plan, prepare, and serve meals in clinics, schools, nursing homes, and hospitals. They help prevent and treat illnesses by teaching clients to eat properly. Some specialize in helping overweight or critically ill patients, or in caring for kidney or diabetic patients. Those supervising kitchen workers may be on their feet most of the day in a hot, steamy kitchen. Some are self-employed and act as consultants.

SOMETHING EXTRA

What's your favorite food? Is it a healthy, low-fat salad, or a big, greasy burger with fries? The food we eat affects our lives in countless ways. Currently about 65 percent of American adults are overweight, and bad eating habits can lead to obesity, low energy and fatigue, diabetes, heart disease, and certain kinds of cancer. Learning to eat healthy foods now will make a huge difference in your life today and tomorrow.

Subjects to Study

Health, nutrition, family and consumer sciences, biology, chemistry, English, accounting

Discover More

Plan and help prepare a healthy, low-fat meal for your family for each day of the week. Be sure to include grains, fruits, vegetables, dairy products, and foods with protein.

Related Jobs

Food service managers, health educators, registered nurses

Education & Training
Bachelor's degree

Earnings
$$$$

Job Outlook
Average increase

Occupational Therapists

On the Job

Occupational therapists help people with disabilities or injuries to become independent and productive. They may help a patient learn to use a wheelchair or work on a new skill. They may help patients find jobs and develop job skills. They usually work in hospitals, schools, or rehab centers. Some provide home health care. The job can be tiring, and therapists must sometimes lift patients and move heavy equipment.

SOMETHING EXTRA

Occupational therapists work in all kinds of settings, from nursing homes to hospitals. But did you know that they also work in preschools? Many work with developmentally delayed children, helping kids make up lost time to get them ready for school. This work might involve helping children play games that challenge their abilities, work puzzles, and learn to use crayons and scissors.

Subjects to Study

Biology, chemistry, physics, health, art, psychology, English, foreign languages

Discover More

Volunteer at a local nursing home to help with activities. You might teach a stroke victim to knit, read to a person whose sight is fading, or visit someone whose family is far away.

Related Jobs

Athletic trainers, physical therapists, recreational therapists, respiratory therapists, speech-language pathologists

Education & Training
Master's degree

Earnings
$$$$$

Job Outlook
Rapid increase

Optometrists

On the Job

Optometrists examine people's eyes to diagnose vision problems and eye diseases. They prescribe glasses and contact lenses and treat certain eye disorders. Some optometrists work especially with the elderly or children. Others develop ways to protect workers' eyes from on-the-job strain or injury. Many are self-employed and work evenings and weekends to fit their patients' schedules.

SOMETHING EXTRA

We all know that in the future (if the movies are right) we will be using lasers to zap each other. But medical professionals are already using lasers to treat patients. In LASIK eye surgery, doctors use a laser to vaporize a portion of your cornea—the clear covering over the front of your eye—to reshape it, ultimately resulting in clearer vision.

Subjects to Study

Physics, chemistry, biology, anatomy, psychology, speech, math

Discover More

With your teacher, contact a local optometrist and ask him or her to visit your school, talk about the job, and do a basic vision screening.

Related Jobs

Chiropractors, dentists, physicians and surgeons, podiatrists, psychologists, veterinarians

Education & Training
Professional degree

Earnings
$$$$$

Job Outlook
Rapid increase

Pharmacists

On the Job

Pharmacists measure and sell medication to people when a doctor says they need it. They must know about the correct use, composition, and effects of drugs. They tell patients about medicines, including reactions and possible side effects, and answer questions. Those in hospitals and clinics advise doctors and nurses on drugs and their effects. Most pharmacists spend much of the workday on their feet. They may wear gloves and safety masks when handling drugs. Many work nights and weekends.

SOMETHING EXTRA

A big part of a pharmacist's job is answering questions. Because many pharmacists work with the public, these might range from "Can I take this cold remedy with this pain reliever?" to "How do I get rid of this wart?" Their special knowledge makes them the expert for patients and doctors alike. In fact, several cases have been reported of pharmacists catching doctors' errors, often with life-saving effects.

Subjects to Study

Math, biology, chemistry, physics, social sciences, English, foreign languages

Discover More

Talk to a pharmacist and ask about the training needed for this job. Ask how he or she keeps up with new drugs that hit the market every day. Then, just for fun, ask about the most ridiculous question he or she has ever been asked on the job.

Related Jobs

Biological scientists, medical scientists, pharmacy technicians and aides, physicians and surgeons, registered nurses

Education & Training
Professional degree

Earnings
$$$$$

Job Outlook
Above-average increase

Physical Therapists

On the Job

Physical therapists work with accident victims, stroke patients, and people with disabilities. They evaluate patients and make plans to help them recover their physical abilities and relieve pain. They may use electricity, heat, or cold to relieve pain, reduce swelling, or increase flexibility. They work in hospitals, clinics, and private offices. Physical therapists must be strong enough to move patients and heavy equipment.

SOMETHING EXTRA

Have you ever heard the term *passive exercise?* It's not some new weight-loss miracle; it's simply a way physical therapists can help patients who have not been able to move their muscles for a long time. The therapist stretches the patient's joints and muscles to build flexibility. Gradually, the patient begins to move his or her own muscles. The patient can then begin to exercise with weights.

Subjects to Study

Biology, chemistry, physics, psychology, anatomy, English, foreign languages

Discover More

Talk to the gym teacher at your school about this kind of work. Ask him or her to help you put together an exercise plan to help you build your own strength and endurance.

Related Jobs

Audiologists, chiropractors, occupational therapists, recreational therapists, speech-language pathologists

Education & Training
Master's degree

Earnings
$$$$$

Job Outlook
Rapid increase

Physician Assistants

On the Job

Physician assistants always work under the supervision of a physician. They handle many of the routine but time-consuming tasks physicians do, such as taking medical records, examining patients, and ordering X-rays and tests. They also treat minor injuries. They often work weekends and evenings and may make house calls or go to nursing homes to check on patients. Physician assistants are usually on their feet for long periods.

SOMETHING EXTRA

In many small, rural communities in the United States, medical doctors are in short supply. Some communities have no resident doctors at all. In such communities, physician assistants (PAs) are the primary health-care providers. They see patients on a day-to-day basis, handling routine office visits. A doctor visits the clinic one or two days a week, though the PA can call the doctor for advice or in emergencies.

Subjects to Study

Biology, chemistry, math, psychology, English, foreign languages, anatomy, nutrition

Discover More

To learn more about this job, check out the Web site of the American Academy of Physician Assistants: www.aapa.org.

Related Jobs

Audiologists, occupational therapists, physical therapists, registered nurses, speech-language pathologists

Education & Training
Master's degree

Earnings
$$$$$

Job Outlook
Rapid increase

Physicians & Surgeons

On the Job

Physicians help people who are sick or have been hurt. They examine patients, perform tests, prescribe treatments, and teach people about health care. Surgeons perform operations on patients with illness and injuries. Physicians work in hospitals, clinics, and private practice. Many work 60 hours a week or more. They may be on call for emergency visits to the hospital. Most doctors travel frequently from their offices to hospitals to care for patients.

SOMETHING EXTRA

When a woman goes into labor in the middle of the night, who does she call? Her doctor! Obstetricians often work as part of a group practice so that they can share the work of delivering babies who arrive after hours and on weekends and holidays. Each night of the week, a different doctor is on call to deliver babies and handle emergencies. That way, obstetricians get some nights to spend at home with their own families.

Subjects to Study

Physics, chemistry, biology, psychology, health, nutrition, English, math

Discover More

Call your local hospital and ask about volunteer opportunities. Many have programs that let young people visit with or read to patients, deliver packages, greet visitors, and help with the library cart.

Related Jobs

Chiropractors, dentists, optometrists, physician assistants, podiatrists, registered nurses, veterinarians

Education & Training
Professional degree

Earnings
$$$$$

Job Outlook
Rapid increase

Podiatrists

On the Job

Podiatrists diagnose and treat diseases and injuries of the foot and lower leg. They may treat corns, calluses, ingrown toenails, bunions, and arch problems. They also treat ankle and foot injuries, deformities, and infections. They take care of foot problems caused by diseases such as diabetes. They prescribe medications and order physical therapy. They set broken bones and perform surgery. Podiatrists usually run their own small businesses, but they may visit patients in nursing homes and perform surgeries at hospitals.

SOMETHING EXTRA

Did you know that one in four Americans has foot problems? And women are four times as likely as men to have serious foot problems! The culprit? Those elegant high-heeled shoes. That's why experts recommend that women wear high heels only occasionally. For everyday wear, doctors recommend sensible, wide-toed, flat shoes or tennis shoes.

Subjects to Study

Biology, chemistry, physics, anatomy, health, English

Discover More

For more information on this job, see the careers section of the Web site for the American Podiatric Medical Association: www.apma.org/careers.htm.

Related Jobs

Athletic trainers, chiropractors, massage therapists, occupational therapists, physical therapists, physicians and surgeons

Education & Training
Professional degree

Earnings
$$$$$

Job Outlook
Average increase

Radiation Therapists

On the Job

Radiation therapists use machines to administer radiation treatment to cancer patients. The machines project high-energy X-rays that shrink and sometimes destroy cancerous cells. Therapists advise patients and perform the treatment. They most often work in hospitals and cancer treatment centers. Great care is taken to prevent overexposure to the radiation.

Subjects to Study

English, anatomy, psychology, physics, chemistry, biology

Discover More

To learn more about radiation therapy and the work therapists perform, visit the National Cancer Institute's Web site at www.cancer.gov/cancerinfo/radiation-therapy-and-you.

Related Jobs

Cardiovascular technologists and technicians, dental hygienists, diagnostic medical sonographers, nuclear medicine technicians, nursing and psychiatric aides, physical therapist assistants and aides, radiologic technologists and technicians, registered nurses

Education & Training
Associate degree

Earnings
$$$$$

Job Outlook
Rapid increase

Recreational Therapists

On the Job

Recreational therapists help people with medical problems improve their health and well-being. They teach patients games, arts and crafts, dance, music, and sports activities. These activities help patients regain skills they've lost because of illness or injury and improve their state of mind. They work closely with medical staff in hospitals and nursing homes. They must be strong enough to move patients and equipment and to participate in activities.

Subjects to Study

English, speech, communication skills, anatomy, psychology, health, art, music, dance, physical education

Discover More

Volunteer some time each week at a nursing home in your neighborhood. Ask the activities director whether you can help him or her plan and carry out activities for the residents. You might help with an art project, read to a patient, or call out numbers in the bingo game.

Related Jobs

Counselors, occupational therapists, physical therapists, speech-language pathologists, teachers—special education

Education & Training
Bachelor's degree

Earnings
$$$

Job Outlook
Above-average increase

Registered Nurses

On the Job

Registered nurses care for the sick and injured and help people stay well. In clinics, hospitals, and nursing homes, they provide much of the day-to-day care for patients, under a doctor's supervision. They take patient histories, give shots and medicines, and teach patients about helping with their own care. Some assist in surgeries. Nurses work nights, weekends, and holidays, and they often work long shifts. They must be able to cope with emergencies and high stress.

SOMETHING EXTRA

You might know that nurses help doctors, but did you know that if you have surgery, your life might depend on one? According to several studies, hospitals with more registered nurses have lower death rates following surgeries than those with fewer nurses. That's because it's often a nurse who notices if a patient has a bad reaction to a drug or complications from surgery. It's a fact: Nurses save lives.

Subjects to Study

Health, biology, chemistry, physics, anatomy, psychology, nutrition, English, foreign languages

Discover More

A good way to learn about working in the medical field is to volunteer at a hospital or nursing home. You might organize activities, visit with patients, deliver supplies, or help with basic patient care.

Related Jobs

Dental hygienists, diagnostic medical sonographers, emergency medical technicians and paramedics, licensed practical and licensed vocational nurses, physician assistants

Education & Training
Associate degree

Earnings
$$$$

Job Outlook
Rapid increase

Respiratory Therapists

On the Job

Respiratory therapists care for patients with breathing problems, from premature babies to heart attack victims. They perform tests, connect patients to machines that help with breathing, and teach patients how to use these machines at home. Therapists may help in surgery by removing mucus from a patient's lungs so that he or she can breathe more easily. Those in hospitals spend most of their time on their feet. They must be able to work calmly in emergencies.

Subjects to Study

Health, biology, chemistry, anatomy, physics, English

Discover More

Asthma is on the rise in the United States, especially among children. Talk to someone who has asthma and find out what type of medicine or therapy he or she uses to prevent or treat asthma attacks.

Related Jobs

Athletic trainers, cardiovascular technologists and technicians, diagnostic medical sonographers, nuclear medicine technologists, occupational therapists, physical therapists, radiation therapists, radiologic technologists and technicians, registered nurses

Education & Training
Associate degree

Earnings
$$$$

Job Outlook
Rapid increase

Speech-Language Pathologists

On the Job

Sometimes called speech therapists, speech-language pathologists work with people who cannot speak well. They teach patients how to improve their language skills. They may teach sign language to non-speaking patients, and they work with people who have swallowing difficulties. Some do research on how people communicate.

SOMETHING EXTRA

People who stutter often can speak and sing more smoothly when they speak as part of a group, such as in a choir or when reciting the Pledge of Allegiance. Scientists used this fact to invent a device that helps people who stutter. It looks like a small hearing aid that is worn in the ear. The aid makes it sound to the person like he or she is speaking in a group, so he or she can speak more fluently.

Subjects to Study

English, foreign languages, speech, biology, chemistry, physics, psychology

Discover More

Speech therapists help clients learn to speak clearly. Practice your speaking skills by recording yourself while reading. Play back the recording and listen to your speaking skills. Are you clear and understandable? If not, practice speaking in front of a mirror and watch how you make the sounds.

Related Jobs

Audiologists, occupational therapists, physical therapists, psychologists, recreational therapists

Education & Training
Master's degree

Earnings
$$$$

Job Outlook
Above-average increase

Veterinarians

On the Job

Veterinarians care for pets, farm animals, zoo residents, and laboratory animals. They set broken bones, treat injuries, prescribe medicine, perform surgery, and vaccinate animals against diseases. They teach people how to care for animals. Most veterinarians treat animals in private clinics or hospitals and work 50 hours or more a week. They may work nights and weekends. Those treating large animals travel to farms or ranches to see their patients. A number of veterinarians engage in research.

SOMETHING EXTRA

What happens when an elephant at the zoo has a stomachache? Or the giraffe has a sore throat? Or the lion needs a tooth pulled? Most zoos have on-staff veterinarians to care for their animals. These doctors plan the diet and exercise programs for all kinds of animals—from monkeys and flamingoes to sharks and lizards. They supervise breeding programs and, when necessary, perform surgery. Zoo vets probably have the most diverse client list in the world!

Subjects to Study

Biology, chemistry, physics, zoology, English

Discover More

Visit an animal shelter and talk to the workers about volunteer opportunities. Some shelters let volunteers come in to feed, bathe, play with, and pet the animals.

Related Jobs

Animal care and service workers, biological scientists, chiropractors, dentists, medical scientists, optometrists, physicians and surgeons, podiatrists, veterinary technologists and technicians

Education & Training
Professional degree

Earnings
$$$$$

Job Outlook
Rapid increase

Athletic Trainers

On the Job

Athletic trainers specialize in the prevention and treatment of injuries to muscles and bones, most often related to sports, training, or exercising. They are heavily involved in the rehabilitation process. They work in hospitals and clinics and with college and professional sports teams. Many of them work long hours, and night and weekend work is common.

SOMETHING EXTRA

Injuries are common in sports—there simply is no avoiding them. Sprains, strains, bruises, and scrapes are a dime a dozen, but the more serious injuries can often be avoided with the proper training and equipment. The two most common sites for sports injuries are the ankles and knees. Thus it is always important to have the right shoes, guards, and braces, and not to overstress your body by pushing too hard.

Subjects to Study

Health, physical education, biology, anatomy, physics, chemistry

Discover More

If your school has sports teams, it probably has an athletic trainer that it consults in case of injury or for education. See if you can interview that person and ask him or her what training was required for the job.

Related Jobs

Chiropractors, emergency medical technicians and paramedics, licensed practical and licensed vocational nurses, massage therapists, occupational therapists, physical therapists, physician assistants, physicians and surgeons, podiatrists, recreational therapists, registered nurses, respiratory therapists

Education & Training
Bachelor's degree

Earnings
$$$

Job Outlook
Rapid increase

Cardiovascular Technologists & Technicians

On the Job

Cardiovascular technologists and technicians help doctors treat heart and blood vessel diseases. They use a variety of tests, monitor the results, prepare patients for procedures, and sometimes assist in surgery. They may schedule patient appointments, type doctors' reports, keep patient files, and care for the testing equipment. They usually work in hospitals and clinics and may work evenings and weekends.

SOMETHING EXTRA

Doctors often ask for an EKG (electrocardiogram) test before an operation or as part of a physical exam. A cardiovascular technician administers an EKG by attaching electrodes to a patient's arms, chest, and legs. A machine records the heart's electrical impulses. Another common practice is the stress test, in which the patient walks on a treadmill while the technician monitors his or her EKG test.

Subjects to Study

Communication skills, math, computer skills, health, biology, anatomy

Discover More

Talk to an EKG supervisor or a cardiologist at your local hospital. Ask a technician about on-the-job training opportunities in your area. The hospital staff can tell you more about this job.

Related Jobs

Diagnostic medical sonographers, nuclear medicine technologists, radiation therapists, radiologic technologists and technicians, respiratory therapists

Education & Training
Associate degree

Earnings
$$$$

Job Outlook
Rapid increase

Clinical Laboratory Technologists & Technicians

On the Job

These workers do medical tests to help detect, diagnose, and treat diseases. They match blood types, test for drug levels, and look for abnormal cells. They analyze test results and send them to doctors. Special equipment allows them to do more than one test at a time. They may work nights and weekends. They wear gloves and masks to protect themselves from infections and diseases.

SOMETHING EXTRA

Cancer is a deadly disease, but today's screening tests are helping doctors win the war against this killer. Pap smears detect cervical cancer, mammograms find breast cancer, and biopsies help determine whether suspicious tissues are cancerous. After the doctor administers the test, he or she sends it to a lab for analysis. It is the lab technician who tests the samples and decides whether they are cancerous. These workers are in the business of saving lives.

Subjects to Study

Biology, chemistry, physics, computer skills, math

Discover More

Rub slices of white bread against different surfaces: a trash can, your hair, the inside of your desk, the floor, dirt, whatever. Seal each piece in a plastic bag with a label telling what it touched. Let the bags sit for a week, then look at them through a magnifying glass. Which surface generated the most mold? Important: When you're finished, throw the bags away without opening them. Mold can make you sick!

Related Jobs

Chemists and materials scientists, science technicians, veterinary technologists and technicians

Education & Training
Associate degree to Bachelor's degree

Earnings
$$$

Job Outlook
Above-average increase

Dental Hygienists

On the Job

Dental hygienists examine patients' teeth and gums to find disease. They help dentists by cleaning patients' teeth, taking and developing X-rays, and applying fluoride treatments. They teach patients how to brush and floss their teeth correctly. Many work part-time for more than one dentist, and they often work on weekends and evenings. They wear gloves and masks to protect themselves from diseases.

Subjects to Study

Biology, chemistry, health, nutrition, anatomy, English, foreign languages

Discover More

Dentists contend that flossing is just as important as brushing and recommend doing it at least once a day. Take an anonymous survey of your class and other classes, asking how often people brush and floss their teeth. The results might surprise you. Better yet, they might make you want to become a dental hygienist.

Related Jobs

Dental assistants, medical assistants, occupational therapist assistants and aides, physical therapist assistants and aides, physician assistants, radiation therapists, registered nurses

Education & Training
Associate degree

Earnings
$$$$$

Job Outlook
Rapid increase

Diagnostic Medical Sonographers

On the Job

Sonographers use special machines that send sound waves through the body to diagnose illness. Doctors use the results of these tests to find tumors, check growing fetuses, and make medical decisions. Sonographers are on their feet for long periods and may have to lift patients. Most work normal hours, although they may be on call for emergencies.

SOMETHING EXTRA

Ultrasounds are very helpful in determining whether a pregnant woman is carrying more than one baby. These images show twins, triplets, and sometimes more fetuses growing inside. Imagine Bobbi McCaughey's surprise in 1997 when an ultrasound revealed seven babies! Mrs. McCaughey was the first woman in recorded history to deliver live septuplets, but her record was short lived as Nkem Chukwu of Texas delivered octuplets only a year later.

Subjects to Study

Health, biology, math, shop courses, computer science, English

Discover More

To learn more about sonography, visit an obstetrician's office and ask to watch an ultrasound. The sonographers use the machine to actually see inside a womb and show images of a growing baby. You might need them to point out key features like eyes and fingers as they go.

Related Jobs

Cardiovascular technologists and technicians, clinical laboratory technologists and technicians, nuclear medicine technologists, radiologic technologists and technicians

Education & Training
Associate degree

Earnings
$$$$

Job Outlook
Above-average increase

Emergency Medical Technicians & Paramedics

On the Job

Emergency medical technicians (EMTs) and paramedics drive ambulances and give emergency medical care. They determine a patient's medical condition at the scene, stabilize the patient, and then drive him or her to the hospital. They work outdoors in all kinds of weather, and the work can be very stressful. Some patients may become violent, and EMTs may be exposed to diseases. They are often on call and work long hours any day of the week.

SOMETHING EXTRA

What's a typical day like for an EMT? There is no such thing! Because EMTs respond to emergencies, their jobs are never the same from day to day. They might be the first on the scene of a car accident in the morning, revive a heart attack victim at lunch, and deliver a baby in a taxicab by dinner. EMTs must be able to remain calm in any situation because they never know what's around the next corner.

Subjects to Study

Driver's education, health, biology, chemistry, anatomy, English, foreign languages

Discover More

Check with the Red Cross in your area to register for a first-aid or CPR course. You can learn how to save another person's life and be helpful in different kinds of emergencies.

Related Jobs

Air traffic controllers, fire fighters, physician assistants, police and detectives, registered nurses

Education & Training
Voc/tech training

Earnings
$$

Job Outlook
Average increase

Licensed Practical & Licensed Vocational Nurses

On the Job

Licensed practical nurses (LPNs) take care of sick and injured people. They are supervised by doctors or registered nurses. They help patients with bathing, dressing, and personal hygiene; feed them; and care for their emotional needs. They keep their patients as comfortable as possible. Licensed vocational nurses (LVNs) are the same as LPNs, except that they are licensed to work in California and Texas. Nurses must be strong enough to lift patients and able to deal with stress.

SOMETHING EXTRA

Some LPNs work as private-duty nurses. Instead of working for a hospital or clinic, these nurses provide in-home care to patients. They may work 8 to 12 hours a day caring for a single patient. In some cases, their duties involve caring for other members of the patient's family as well. At night, most return to their own homes and families, but some live with their patient's family while they provide care.

Subjects to Study

Health, anatomy, psychology, first aid, nutrition, family and consumer sciences, English, foreign languages

Discover More

Licensed practical nursing courses are offered in some high school vocational programs. Talk to your school counselor about these programs and find out whether any are available through high schools in your area.

Related Jobs

Athletic trainers, emergency medical technicians and paramedics, home health aides and personal and home care aides, medical assistants, nursing and psychiatric aides, registered nurses

Education & Training
Voc/tech training

Earnings
$$$

Job Outlook
Rapid increase

Medical Records & Health Information Technicians

On the Job

These workers organize and keep track of patients' medical records. First, they make sure all the right forms have been signed. Then they put the information into a computer file. Finally, they code the information so that it can be pulled up easily. They may work day, evening, or night shifts. Health information technicians must be computer literate and pay close attention to details.

SOMETHING EXTRA

What happens if someone gets hold of your medical records? Well, if your family has a history of cancer, for example, a business might decide not to hire you because you are at risk for high medical bills. Or an insurance company might decide not to sign you up. That's why confidentiality is such a big issue in this job. Health information technicians must be able to keep patients' information private and secure.

Subjects to Study

English, math, computer skills, anatomy, biology

Discover More

The American Health Information Management Association offers an independent-study program for health information technicians. You can e-mail the association at info@ahima.org or check out its Web site at www.ahima.org.

Related Jobs

Medical and health services managers, medical transcriptionists

Education & Training
Associate degree

Earnings
$$

Job Outlook
Rapid increase

Nuclear Medicine Technologists

On the Job

Nuclear medicine technologists give radioactive drugs to patients. These drugs help doctors diagnose and treat diseases. Using a camera, the technologist follows the drug as it enters the patient's body and records the drug's effects using magnetic resonance imaging (MRI). Technologists must keep accurate, detailed patient records. Technologists must also be careful to keep from being exposed to too much radiation. They wear badges that measure radiation levels.

SOMETHING EXTRA

What do doctors do when a child is complaining of bone pain? One answer is to use nuclear medicine to get a clear picture of what's inside the bones. Nuclear medicine is used for cardiac tests, for bone scans, for lung scans, for older people, and for children. Nuclear medicine technologists are the ones who administer the tests. They must have a good rapport with people of all ages so that they can help put patients at ease. After all, the words nuclear and medicine don't sound like a comforting combination!

Subjects to Study

Biology, chemistry, physics, math, computer science

Discover More

You can get more information about this job by e-mailing the Joint Review Committee on Educational Programs in Nuclear Medicine Technology at jrcnmt@coxinet.net. Or visit their Web site at www.jrcnmt.org.

Related Jobs

Cardiovascular technologists and technicians, clinical laboratory technologists and technicians, diagnostic medical sonographers, radiation therapists, radiologic technologists and technicians

Education & Training
Associate degree

Earnings
$$$$$

Job Outlook
Above-average increase

Occupational Health & Safety Specialists

On the Job

These workers help keep workplaces safe and workers healthy. They identify hazardous conditions and practices and make recommendations for fixing them. They check that dangerous materials are stored and used properly. Many are employed by federal, state, or local government agencies to enforce rules on health and safety. Others work for companies to ensure that their workplaces are operating safely.

SOMETHING EXTRA

Have you ever sat at a desk or used a mouse for a long time? Did you start to feel tired or uncomfortable? Imagine sitting in an uncomfortable position for eight hours a day! Ergonomics is the science of fitting equipment to the worker. Occupational health and safety specialists work to make equipment ergonomic. Proper ergonomic design promotes correct body positioning, increases worker comfort, and decreases fatigue. Ergonomics can prevent repetitive strain injuries, which can eventually cause long-term disability.

Subjects to Study

Biology, chemistry, physics, geology, English, computer science

Discover More

Government health and safety specialists use rules established by the Occupational Safety and Health Administration (OSHA), part of the U.S. Department of Labor. You can learn more about OSHA from its Web site: www.osha.gov.

Related Jobs

Agricultural inspectors, construction and building inspectors, occupational health and safety technicians

Education & Training
Bachelor's degree

Earnings
$$$$

Job Outlook
Average increase

Occupational Health & Safety Technicians

On the Job

These workers focus on preventing harm to workers, property, the environment, and the public. For example, they might help design safe work spaces, inspect machines, or test air quality. Some technicians work for governments, conducting safety inspections and imposing fines. They collect data that occupational health and safety specialists then analyze. They help to implement and evaluate safety programs.

SOMETHING EXTRA

On Sept. 11, 2001, the U.S. suffered the most devastating terrorist attack in history. Months later, New York occupational health and safety inspectors were still working at the scene of the World Trade Center collapse, testing air and soil samples and collecting blood samples from rescue and cleanup workers. Their findings were grim. Firefighters, construction workers, and others who spent much time at Ground Zero showed signs of asbestos poisoning, which means that the attack might claim more victims for years to come.

Subjects to Study

Biology, chemistry, physics, geology, English, computer science

Discover More

Take a glass of water from the kitchen sink and hold it to the light. Is the water clear? If it's cloudy, does it clear up in a couple of minutes? What does the water smell like? It may smell slightly like chlorine if you are on your city's water supply. Any other smell may indicate that your water should be tested.

Related Jobs

Agricultural inspectors, construction and building inspectors, fire inspectors and investigators, occupational health and safety specialists

Education & Training
Associate degree

Earnings
$$$$

Job Outlook
Above-average increase

Opticians, Dispensing

On the Job

Dispensing opticians work for eye doctors, making glasses and contact lenses according to the doctors' orders. They keep customer records, track inventory, and help customers find frames that fit them well. Many work evenings and weekends or part-time. They must be careful with the glass-cutting machinery and chemicals they use to make lenses.

SOMETHING EXTRA

When was the first eye surgery performed? Would you guess this century? Or in the 1800s? How about in 1000 B.C.? Long before glasses were invented, ancient surgeons were removing cataracts from people's eyes. Evidence indicates that this surgery was being performed in India more than 3,000 years ago—and probably without anesthesia!

Subjects to Study

Physics, anatomy, algebra, geometry, mechanical drawing

Discover More

Visit an optical store in your community. Look through the wide selection of eyewear and decide which frames best fit you. Use the opportunity to talk to one of the dispensing opticians about this job.

Related Jobs

Jewelers and precious stone and metal workers

Education & Training
Long-term OJT

Earnings
$$$

Job Outlook
Average increase

Pharmacy Technicians & Aides

On the Job

Pharmacy technicians and aides help licensed pharmacists provide medicines and other health-care products to patients. In pharmacies, they measure and prepare medications, handle telephone calls, work the cash register, stock shelves, and perform other clerical duties. They can also work in hospitals and nursing homes, helping to deliver and dispense medicine. They do most of their work standing. They may work nights and weekends, since many pharmacies are open 24 hours a day.

SOMETHING EXTRA

"Can I take this medicine along with an herbal supplement?" "Does this diet drug work?" "My baby is running a fever. What should I give her?" These are the kinds of questions pharmacy workers are asked every day. Because they deal with people who are sick or in pain, pharmacy workers must be patient and helpful. In short, these workers need good people skills!

Subjects to Study

Math, computer skills, chemistry, biology, health, English

Discover More

Visit your local pharmacy and ask the pharmacist if you can observe him or her at work for an hour. How often does the pharmacist interact with customers? How much time is spent filling prescriptions? Ask the pharmacist about training programs for the job.

Related Jobs

Dental assistants, medical assistants, medical records and health information technicians, medical transcriptionists, pharmacists

Education & Training
Short-term OJT to Moderate-term OJT

Earnings
$$

Job Outlook
Rapid increase

Radiologic Technologists & Technicians

On the Job

Radiologic technologists and technicians work in hospitals and clinics. They operate the machines that take X-ray pictures or magnetic resolution pictures of people's bones and internal organs. They must wear badges that measure the amount of radiation they are exposed to on the job. These workers might work nights or weekends and might be on call during odd hours. They are on their feet most of the day and must be strong enough to lift patients.

SOMETHING EXTRA

The first X-ray taken was by a German scientist named Conrad Roentgen, who discovered them quite by accident. He called them X rays (rather than Roentgen rays as his colleagues suggested) because the type of radiation was unknown. The first X-ray of the human body was a picture of his wife's hand, ring and all.

Subjects to Study

Biology, chemistry, physics, math, computer science

Discover More

You can get more information about this job by e-mailing the American Society of Radiologic Technologists at memberservices@asrt.org. Or visit their Web site at www.asrt.org.

Related Jobs

Cardiovascular technologists and technicians, diagnostic medical sonographers, nuclear medicine technologists, respiratory therapists

Education & Training
Associate degree

Earnings
$$$$

Job Outlook
Above-average increase

Surgical Technologists

On the Job

Surgical technologists set up equipment in the operating room, prepare patients for surgery, and take patients to and from the operating room. They help the surgical team "scrub" and put on gloves, masks, and surgical clothing. During an operation, they help with supplies and instruments and operate lights and equipment. After the operation, they restock the operating room. Surgical technicians must be able to stay calm and steady in stressful circumstances.

Subjects to Study

Health, biology, chemistry, math, anatomy, English, foreign languages

Discover More

Surgical technicians must be comfortable dealing with operations of all kinds. One way to test your tolerance for this is to take a biology course in which you dissect an animal. Another way is to watch informational television programs where actual surgeries are performed.

Related Jobs

Clinical laboratory technologists and technicians, dental assistants, licensed practical and licensed vocational nurses, medical assistants

Education & Training
Voc/tech training

Earnings
$$$

Job Outlook
Rapid increase

Veterinary Technologists & Technicians

On the Job

Veterinary technologists and technicians perform many of the same duties for a veterinarian that a nurse would for a physician, including handling laboratory and clinical work such as urine and blood tests. They may work in private vets' offices, zoos, research facilities, and other places where veterinarians work. Some of the work can be unpleasant and even dangerous.

> ### SOMETHING EXTRA
>
> Veterinary technologists and technicians often have to help put sick animals to sleep. It's difficult for them emotionally, but they know that it's usually the kindest thing you can do for an animal that is in pain. It's quick, and the only pain for the animal is the stick from the needle. They also may console the pet's owners on this difficult day.

Subjects to Study

Biology, math, chemistry, zoology, communication skills

Discover More

Volunteer to help out at your local humane society or vet's office. Watch the veterinary technicians at work and see the kinds of things they do to help the vet and the animals. It's often unpleasant work, but you do get to be around animals!

Related Jobs

Animal care and service workers, veterinarians

Education & Training
Associate degree

Earnings
$$

Job Outlook
Rapid increase

Service Occupations

Dental Assistants

On the Job

Dental assistants help dentists during patient exams and treatments. They schedule appointments, keep patient records, handle billing, and order supplies. Those with lab duties clean removable dentures and make temporary crowns for teeth. They wear gloves and masks to protect themselves from diseases and germs. Many work evenings and Saturdays, and they spend a good part of their time on their feet.

SOMETHING EXTRA

Centuries ago people believed that tooth decay was caused by worms in the gums. The only way to remove the decay was to pull the tooth. This was a painful process, because they had no anesthesia to numb the area first. Often, the dentist's assistant had the job of holding the patient down while the dentist yanked out the tooth. Today, dental assistants spend time calming patients' fears instead of pinning them down.

Subjects to Study

Biology, chemistry, health, business courses, math, computer skills, psychology

Discover More

Visit your dentist's office and ask about careers in this field. Does your dentist employ an assistant? What does he or she do? Ask the assistant about training and the job.

Related Jobs

Dental hygienists, medical assistants, occupational therapist assistants and aides, pharmacy technicians and aides, physical therapist assistants and aides, surgical technologists

Education & Training
Moderate-term OJT

Earnings
$$$

Job Outlook
Rapid increase

Home Health Aides & Personal & Home Care Aides

On the Job

These aides help elderly, disabled, and seriously ill patients to live at home instead of in a nursing home. They clean, do laundry, prepare meals, and help with personal needs and hygiene. They also take the patient's pulse and blood pressure and give medication. Aides keep records of each patient's condition and progress. They often work part-time and weekend hours.

SOMETHING EXTRA

When is a pet not a pet? When it's a trained companion for a person with disabilities. Today, some people who are wheelchair-bound have trained monkeys who help them live independently. These little animals perform simple household tasks, fetch items for their owners, dial the phone, and even call for help in an emergency. Trained animals allow their owners to live at home, and they provide companionship and love.

Subjects to Study

Family and consumer sciences, nutrition, health, first aid, English, foreign languages, anatomy, communication skills, psychology

Discover More

Can you help out in your neighbors' homes by cleaning, washing clothes, running errands, shoveling, or doing yard work? You can do these chores as a way to earn money or as a kind act if someone who is ill or elderly needs help.

Related Jobs

Child care workers, licensed practical and licensed vocational nurses, medical assistants, nursing and psychiatric aides, occupational therapist assistants and aides, physical therapist assistants and aides, radiation therapists, registered nurses, social and human services assistants

Education & Training
Short-term OJT

Earnings
$

Job Outlook
Rapid increase

Massage Therapists

On the Job

These therapists use massage to treat muscle pain, relieve stress, rehabilitate sport injuries, and promote general health. Massage therapists can specialize in 80 different types of massage. Some work in hospitals, nursing homes, or sports facilities, although a good number operate out of private offices or travel to homes and businesses. Massage therapy is physically demanding work and requires therapists to be on their feet most of the day.

Subjects to Study

English, psychology, physical education, anatomy, business courses

Discover More

The best way to learn more about massage therapy is to practice it. Start by giving shoulder rubs, because that area is often a source of muscular tension. Be sure to try a variety of motions.

Related Jobs

Athletic trainers, chiropractors, physical therapist assistants and aides, physical therapists

Education & Training
Voc/tech training

Earnings
$$$

Job Outlook
Above-average increase

Young Person's Occupational Outlook Handbook, © JIST Works

Medical Assistants

On the Job

Medical assistants help keep your doctor's office running smoothly. They answer phones, greet patients, schedule appointments, arrange for hospital admissions and tests, handle billing, and file records. They may take medical histories, explain treatments to patients, and help doctors with exams. They may prepare and perform laboratory tests. They must have good people skills. Many work evenings and weekends.

SOMETHING EXTRA

Do you like small children? Does holding a baby make your day? Do people tell you that you have a way with kids? If so, being a medical assistant in a pediatrician's office might be the job for you. Pediatric medical assistants must enjoy children, have a high tolerance for noise and chaos, and love helping people.

Subjects to Study

Math, health, biology, computer skills, office skills, English, foreign languages

Discover More

Ask your own doctor if you can spend a day in the office watching what the medical assistants do. Maybe you can help file papers or make copies.

Related Jobs

Dental assistants, dental hygienists, licensed practical and licensed vocational nurses, medical records and health information technicians, medical secretaries, medical transcriptionists, nursing and psychiatric aides, occupational therapist assistants and aides, pharmacy technicians and aides, physical therapist assistants and aides, surgical technologists

Education & Training
Moderate-term OJT

Earnings
$$

Job Outlook
Rapid increase

Medical Transcriptionists

On the Job

Medical transcriptionists listen to dictated recordings made by doctors and transcribe them into medical reports, letters, and other written materials. They wear a special headset, use a foot pedal to pause the recording when necessary, and type the materials into a computer, editing it for grammar and clarity. Some transcriptionists work in doctors' offices or hospitals, but many work as freelancers from home.

SOMETHING EXTRA

Why would anyone need a written version of what a doctor says during surgery? In long, complex operations, surgeons often talk into a recorder, describing what they are doing and finding. Those recordings are then transcribed and filed. If a complication arises later, the doctor can simply go back to the files and double-check his or her work, looking for clues to the complication.

Subjects to Study

Computer skills, English, anatomy, biology, foreign languages

Discover More

Make a recording of yourself or a friend reading material out loud from a book or magazine. Then try typing the material from the recording without making any mistakes. Even if the person on the recording reads slowly, you'll have to type fast to keep up!

Related Jobs

Court reporters; human resources assistants, except payroll and timekeeping; medical assistants; medical records and health information technicians; receptionists and information clerks; secretaries and administrative assistants

Education & Training
Voc/tech training

Earnings
$$$

Job Outlook
Average increase

Nursing & Psychiatric Aides

On the Job

Nursing and psychiatric aides care for patients in hospitals, nursing homes, and mental health clinics. These workers feed, bathe, and dress patients, help them get in and out of bed, take temperatures and blood pressures, and set up equipment. They report any signs or changes to doctors or nurses. Most work some weekends and evening hours. They must be strong enough to lift and move patients.

SOMETHING EXTRA

Aides in nursing homes and mental health facilities often have more contact with patients than other staff members do. Because patients often spend months or years in these homes, aides build close relationships with them. Many patients see aides as their special friends, and a caring aide can greatly influence a patient's attitude and outlook on life.

Subjects to Study

Health, nutrition, anatomy, communication skills, English, psychology

Discover More

Volunteer at a nursing home in your community. You might be asked to read to patients, make deliveries, help with activities, or just visit with a patient who is lonely.

Related Jobs

Child care workers, home health aides and personal and home care aides, licensed practical and licensed vocational nurses, medical assistants, occupational therapist assistants and aides, registered nurses, social and human service assistants

Education & Training
Short-term OJT to Voc/tech training

Earnings
$

Job Outlook
Above-average increase

Occupational Therapist Assistants & Aides

On the Job

Occupational therapist assistants help therapists in clinics, rehab centers, nursing homes, and home health care programs. They help injured patients regain use of damaged muscles. They might help patients learn to use wheelchairs or other devices. They help mentally disabled patients learn living skills like cooking and keeping a checkbook. Occupational therapy aides keep patient records and set up equipment. These workers must be strong enough to lift and move patients and equipment.

SOMETHING EXTRA

Some people enjoy the 9-to-5 routine. But for many, spending eight hours a day behind a desk would be torture. Occupational therapist assistants who work with mentally disabled adults may travel to several homes and facilities each day, taking clients grocery shopping, teaching them cooking skills, and helping them apply for assistance.

Subjects to Study

Psychology, anatomy, physical education, communication skills, English, health

Discover More

Try teaching younger children an outdoor activity or game. Plan the activity, deciding whether it's appropriate for their age group. Then teach the children how to play. Watch to make sure they play fairly and safely.

Related Jobs

Dental assistants, medical assistants, pharmacy technicians and aides, physical therapist assistants and aides

Education & Training
Short-term OJT to Associate degree

Earnings
$$$

Job Outlook
Rapid increase

Physical Therapist Assistants & Aides

On the Job

Physical therapist assistants help physical therapists care for patients in hospitals, nursing homes, and home health-care programs. They help patients recovering from injuries or disease improve their mobility, relieve pain, and regain muscle use. They may help with exercises, give massages, and apply hot/cold packs. Physical therapy aides keep equipment in good order, move patients to and from the treatment area, and help with record keeping.

SOMETHING EXTRA

When LeBron James pulls a muscle, who does he turn to for help? A sports medicine specialist is a physical therapist specializing in sports-related injuries. These workers help athletes prepare their bodies for competition, and they are on hand during sporting events to help in emergencies. After an injury or illness, they work with an athlete to help him or her rebuild muscle tone and agility. Of course with LeBron's salary, he could probably hire the Surgeon General.

Subjects to Study

Health, anatomy, physical education, communication skills, psychology

Discover More

Ask your gym teacher to show you some exercises you can use to strengthen your muscles. Then teach these exercises to family members or friends. Set up a regular exercise schedule for yourself.

Related Jobs

Dental assistants, medical assistants, nursing and psychiatric aides, occupational therapist assistants and aides, pharmacy technicians and aides

Education & Training
Short-term OJT to Associate degree

Earnings
$$$

Job Outlook
Rapid increase

Correctional Officers

On the Job

Correctional officers guard people who are awaiting trial and those who have been convicted of crimes. They keep order and enforce rules in jails or prisons and assign and supervise inmates' work. They help inmates with personal problems and report bad behavior. To prevent escapes, they stand guard in towers and at gates. They work indoors and outdoors under very stressful and potentially dangerous conditions. Many work nights and weekends. These workers must be strong and able to use firearms.

Subjects to Study

Physical education, driver's education, psychology, sociology

Discover More

Some state prisons give tours to the public or to school groups. Check to see whether you can visit one to learn more about this job.

Related Jobs

Police and detectives, probation officers and correctional treatment specialists, security guards and gaming surveillance officers

Education & Training
Moderate-term OJT to Work experience

Earnings
$$$

Job Outlook
Average increase

Fire Fighters

On the Job

Fire fighters protect people from the dangers of fires. They must stay physically fit and strong. At the scene of a fire, they rescue victims, perform emergency medical aid, and operate and maintain equipment. During their shifts, fire fighters live at the fire station. Most work 50 hours a week or more. Forest fire fighters may parachute into a fire area to put out fires and dig a fire line. Fire fighting is one of the most dangerous jobs in the economy.

SOMETHING EXTRA

Fire fighters who battle wildfires are a special breed. During the hot, dry months of late summer, they travel from state to state, helping local fire fighters battle forest fires. They may jump from planes into a fire zone to dig fire lines. If a fire travels too quickly and they get trapped, they drop to the ground and cover themselves with a special fireproofed tent. They wait until the fire has passed over them, get up, and keep on fighting the flames.

Subjects to Study

Physical science, chemistry, driver's education, physical education

Discover More

Tour the fire station in your neighborhood. Ask the fire fighters about their jobs, the training they receive, and the risks of the job. Then ask them if you can slide down the pole.

Related Jobs

Emergency medical technicians and paramedics, fire inspectors and investigators, police and detectives

Education & Training
Long-term OJT to
Work experience

Earnings
$$$$

Job Outlook
Above-average
increase

Police & Detectives

On the Job

Police and detectives protect people from crime and violence. They patrol highways, issue traffic tickets, and help accident victims. They collect evidence and investigate crimes. Police detectives often testify in court about their cases. Most work some evenings and weekends. Police work is dangerous and stressful.

SOMETHING EXTRA

The top law enforcement officers in the United States are the special agents of the Federal Bureau of Investigation or FBI. These top cops investigate crimes such as bank robberies, terrorism, kidnapping, drug smuggling, and spying. Special agents train at the FBI Academy in Virginia and are then assigned to a field office, usually not anywhere near their hometowns.

Subjects to Study

English, psychology, sociology, chemistry, physics, driver's education, physical education, foreign languages

Discover More

Police officers often check for fingerprints at the scene of a crime. Make your own fingerprinting kit with talcum powder, a paintbrush, and a magnifying glass. Dust the powder lightly on a solid, shiny surface such as a doorknob. Blow gently. The powder will blow away, except where the greasy marks are. Brush the powdered spots lightly with the paintbrush and examine the prints with the glass.

Education & Training
Long-term OJT to Associate degree

Earnings
$$$$

Related Jobs

Correctional officers, emergency medical technicians and paramedics, fire fighters, private detectives and investigators, probation officers and correctional treatment specialists, security guards and gaming surveillance officers

Job Outlook
Average increase

Private Detectives & Investigators

On the Job

Private detectives and investigators work for lawyers, insurance companies, and other kinds of businesses. They gather information for trials, track down people who owe companies money, and conduct background checks. Some are self-employed and specialize in searching for missing persons or finding information for divorce cases. They may spend long hours watching a person or place, hunting for clues, and interviewing people. They often travel and work irregular hours, and the work may be dangerous.

SOMETHING EXTRA

Say "private detective" and many people think of macho movie detectives in trench coats. But did you know that many detectives these days are women? A detective's greatest asset is an ability to blend into the background, so detective agencies often use women to investigate other women. These female sleuths can follow suspects into gyms, shopping malls, and even restrooms without calling attention to themselves.

Subjects to Study

English, psychology, sociology, chemistry, physics, driver's education, physical education, foreign languages

Discover More

An investigator's main job is collecting information. Use your investigative skills to find interesting information about this job. What can you find at the library or on the Internet that you didn't know before?

Related Jobs

Accountants and auditors; appraisers, examiners, and investigators; bill and account collectors; claims adjusters; financial analysts and personal financial advisors; police and detectives; security guards and gaming surveillance officers

Education & Training
Work experience

Earnings
$$$

Job Outlook
Rapid increase

Security Guards & Gaming Surveillance Officers

On the Job

Guards protect property from fire, theft, vandalism, and break-ins. They patrol the area, usually on foot, or check people entering and leaving the area. Guards may carry a nightstick or gun. Most work some nights and weekends, and the work can be dangerous. Gaming surveillance officers work in casinos and gaming parlors, watching for people who are trying to cheat the system.

SOMETHING EXTRA

Do people call you independent? Do you like being by yourself? Security guards often work alone for hours—especially those who work as night watchmen. To provide these workers with some protection, businesses sometimes give their night guards transmitters. The guards use these devices to maintain contact with a central station. If the guard does not check in at the expected times, or if he or she doesn't respond to a call, the station sends someone to check on him or her.

Subjects to Study

English, driver's education, psychology, physical education, communication skills, computer skills

Discover More

Call a security company in your area and ask if you can speak with someone who hires security guards. Ask that person about the skills you would need to be a guard. Does the company provide training?

Related Jobs

Correctional officers, gaming services occupations, police and detectives, private detectives and investigators

Education & Training
Short-term OJT to Moderate-term OJT

Earnings
$

Job Outlook
Above-average increase

Chefs, Head Cooks & Food Preparation & Serving Supervisors

On the Job

Chefs and head cooks oversee the daily food operation of restaurants and other establishments. They plan meals, supervise other workers, order supplies, set schedules, and develop menus. They use their creativity and knowledge of food to prepare recipes. Kitchens can be crowded and hot. These workers are under pressure to get quality meals prepared quickly.

SOMETHING EXTRA

Did you know that not all chefs work in restaurants? Some work for airlines and cruise ships, planning menus for on-board meals. Some are self-employed, operating their own catering companies. Many celebrities—from Oprah Winfrey to Christina Aguilera—employ private chefs to cook for them. But the most prestigious cooking group might be those who prepare meals for kings and queens, prime ministers, and presidents. These elite chefs even have their own club!

Subjects to Study

Family and consumer sciences, nutrition, math, health, communication skills

Discover More

Cook a three-course meal for your family. Ask a parent to help you look through cookbooks or recipe Web sites. Be sure to pick an appetizer, a main course, and a dessert. Of course you may need some help from other members of the family to put it all together.

Related Jobs

Cooks and food preparation workers, food and beverage serving and related workers, food processing occupations, food service managers

Education & Training
Work experience

Earnings
$$

Job Outlook
Little change

Cooks & Food Preparation Workers

On the Job

These workers prepare, season, and cook a wide range of foods, including soups, salads, main dishes, and desserts. Cooks make food and meals according to recipes. Food preparation workers assist cooks by peeling and cutting vegetables, trimming meat, and keeping work areas clean. All of these workers must fix meals quickly and follow safety and sanitation guidelines. They work in restaurants and other places where food is served, such as schools and hospitals.

> ## SOMETHING EXTRA
>
> Cooking shows depict delicious foods prepared easily and quickly. But behind each dish are more than a dozen people. Some test the recipes. Others chop, measure, and mix. Helpers hide the brand-name labels on cans and jars. Still others fix the same recipe to film at different stages of completion. And who cleans up? You can't have too many cooks in TV kitchens!

Subjects to Study

Family and consumer sciences, nutrition, health

Discover More

Do you help out with the cooking at home? If not, try it! Perhaps you can gather the needed food items, measure ingredients, stir food, add seasonings, and organize the cooking area. To really make the cook happy, help with the cleanup.

Related Jobs

Chefs, head cooks, and food preparation and serving supervisors; food and beverage serving and related workers; food service managers

Education & Training
Short-term OJT to Long-term OJT

Earnings
$

Job Outlook
Little change

Food & Beverage Serving & Related Workers

On the Job

Food and beverage service workers deal with customers in restaurants. They take food orders, fill drink orders, serve food, prepare the bill, and may accept payment. Other workers clean dirty tables and reset them with silverware and napkins. These workers spend hours on their feet. They carry heavy trays and must serve customers quickly and courteously. Most work evenings and weekends, and many work part time.

SOMETHING EXTRA

Working in a restaurant is a time-honored first job for many people. Because the hours are flexible, many aspiring actors and actresses take restaurant jobs while they wait for their big breaks. Movie actors Brad Pitt, Kevin Bacon, and Jennifer Aniston all waited tables while they auditioned in Hollywood. Comedian Drew Carey worked in a Denny's restaurant. And Sandra Bullock worked as a bartender. In fact, about 1 in 10 Americans will work at a McDonald's at some point in their lives.

Subjects to Study

English, foreign languages, math, speech, family and consumer sciences, communication skills

Discover More

The best way to learn about the restaurant industry is to work in it. Look for a part-time job at a fast-food restaurant. Or talk to friends who have worked in one. Find out what they liked and disliked about the job. What hours and days did they work? How much did they make in tips, if any?

Education & Training
Short-term OJT

Earnings
$

Related Jobs

Cashiers; chefs, head cooks, and food preparation and serving supervisors; cooks and food preparation workers; flight attendants; retail salespersons

Job Outlook
Average increase

Building Cleaning Workers

On the Job

Building cleaning workers keep offices, schools, hospitals, hotels, and other buildings clean and in good condition. They clean, repair, empty trash cans, paint, and mow lawns. Cleaning supervisors assign jobs, supervise workers, and order supplies. These people often work evenings and weekends. The work can be dirty and strenuous.

SOMETHING EXTRA

What would you do if you found a diamond ring under a pillow? Or a suitcase full of cash in a closet? Or a small child in the bathroom? If you're a hotel housekeeper, you might just shrug your shoulders and call the front desk. These workers routinely find expensive, unusual, and downright bizarre things in the rooms they clean. People in a hurry to pack up and get on the road are apt to leave behind anything—even their child!

Subjects to Study

Shop courses, family and consumer sciences, physical education

Discover More

Talk to a janitor at your school. Make a list of all the chores and different tasks he or she does. What is the best part of the job? What is the worst part of the job?

Related Jobs

Grounds maintenance workers

Education & Training
Short-term OJT to Work experience

Earnings
$

Job Outlook
Little change

Young Person's Occupational Outlook Handbook, © JIST Works

Grounds Maintenance Workers

On the Job

Grounds maintenance workers care for lawns, trees, gardens, and other plants and keep the grounds free of litter. They may prune, feed, and water gardens and mow and water lawns at private homes and public places. They maintain athletic fields, golf courses, cemeteries, and parks. They work outside in all kinds of weather. Many are self-employed and work seasonally.

SOMETHING EXTRA

Are you happiest when you're outside? Does your perfect day involve sunshine, fresh air, and hard work? Do you like using your muscles and your mind together? If so, landscaping work might be just what you're looking for. These workers plant, prune, weed, and mow to make public areas beautiful. If your green thumb is your pride and joy, this could be the job for you.

Subjects to Study

Biology, zoology, botany, driver's education, business math

Discover More

Plant some flowers around your home or in a pot inside. Start with some easy annuals like snapdragons, petunias, or marigolds. Next, try something trickier, like orchids or roses. Can you make your flowers grow?

Related Jobs

Agricultural workers; farmers, ranchers, and agricultural managers; forest and conservation workers; landscape architects; logging workers

Education & Training
Short-term OJT to Work experience

Earnings
$$

Job Outlook
Above-average increase

Pest Control Workers

On the Job

Pest control workers find and kill roaches, rats, mice, spiders, termites, ants, bees—all kinds of pests that invade people's homes and offices. They use chemicals, poisonous fumes, traps, and electrical equipment to eliminate pests. They travel to homes and offices to perform their work, often crawling and climbing into tight places. They wear protective gear, including respirators, gloves, and goggles. Some work evenings and weekends.

SOMETHING EXTRA

Did you ever wonder what all the chemicals we use do to our environment? That question has prompted interest in organic pesticides. Scientists are developing pesticides using natural ingredients, such as the oils from pennyroyal and eucalyptus plants, cayenne pepper, garlic, peppermint leaves, grasshopper spores, rapeseed, canola oil, and baking soda. Their recipes might not make good salad dressings, but they are far easier on the environment than DDT and other man-made chemicals.

Subjects to Study

Biology, chemistry, zoology, physical education, computer skills, math

Discover More

Learn more about the bugs that inhabit your state by starting a bug collection. Find as many different kinds of insects as possible, then mount them on heavy-duty white cardboard using straight pins. Identify them using a field guide from the library. Label each specimen and learn about its habitat, food, and natural prey.

Education & Training
Moderate-term OJT

Earnings
$$

Related Jobs

Building cleaning workers; construction laborers; grounds maintenance workers; heating, air-conditioning, and refrigeration mechanics and installers

Job Outlook
Above-average increase

Animal Care & Service Workers

On the Job

Animal care and service workers feed, water, bathe, and exercise animals in clinics, kennels, and zoos. They play with the animals, watch for illness or injury, and clean and repair their cages. Kennel staff care for cats and dogs; stable workers groom, exercise, and care for horses; and zookeepers care for wild and exotic animals. They may work outdoors in all kinds of weather. The work can be dirty and dangerous. Many work weekends and nights. Some travel with animals to sports events or shows.

SOMETHING EXTRA

Feeding the animals in a zoo can be a challenge. Zookeepers must know what kind of food the animals need, how much they need, and when to feed them. They must be very careful feeding animals such as lions, tigers, and alligators. Exotic animals might need special foods that must be specially ordered or grown. Zookeepers must plan menus for hundreds of picky eaters on a daily basis—just like preschool workers!

Subjects to Study

Life sciences, zoology, biology, chemistry, physical education

Discover More

You can learn more about this occupation by volunteering at a zoo or animal shelter. You might play with or cuddle small animals, clean cages, put out food and water, or take animals for walks.

Related Jobs

Agricultural workers; biological scientists; farmers, ranchers, and agricultural managers; medical scientists; veterinarians; veterinary assistants and laboratory animal caretakers; veterinary technologists and technicians

Education & Training
Short-term OJT to Moderate-term OJT

Earnings
$

Job Outlook
Rapid increase

Barbers, Cosmetologists & Other Personal Appearance Workers

On the Job

These workers help people look their best. They cut, shampoo, style, color, and perm hair. They may fit customers for hairpieces, shave male customers, and give facial massages and advice on makeup. Many cosmetologists are trained to give manicures. They keep customer records and order supplies. These workers spend a lot of time on their feet. Many work part time, and many are self-employed.

SOMETHING EXTRA

In Hollywood's "beauty wars," any small advantage can mean the difference between getting a role and going broke. That's why actors and actresses change their hairstyles, their wardrobes, and their looks so often. Hairstylists in Tinseltown must stay current with the latest looks and trends. A stylist who caters to the newest stars' whims can become almost as well known and wealthy as the stars themselves.

Subjects to Study

Communication skills, business courses, accounting, speech, health

Discover More

Set up a hair salon at home and practice on yourself or a friend. Look through magazines for the latest styles. Then wash and style your friend's hair.

Related Jobs

Fitness workers, massage therapists

Education & Training
Short-term OJT to Voc/tech training

Earnings
$

Job Outlook
Rapid increase

Child Care Workers

On the Job

Child care workers care for children under the age of five. Those watching infants and toddlers may change diapers, heat bottles, and rock children to sleep. Those caring for pre-schoolers serve meals, play games, read stories, and organize activities to help the children socialize and learn skills. A third of these workers run child care services out of their homes. The work can be tiring. Workers must be strong enough to lift and move children.

SOMETHING EXTRA

Have you ever walked into a day-care center? Often, the scene looks like barely controlled chaos. Young children don't sit at desks and color quietly. They shout, dance, cartwheel, run, and sing out loud. That's how they learn. It takes a special kind of person to work with children this age. Child care workers must be creative, patient, and calm, and have a healthy sense of humor!

Subjects to Study

English, child development, psychology, family and consumer sciences, art, music, drama, health, speech

Discover More

The easiest way to learn about this job is to baby-sit or help someone else take care of young children. It's also a good way to pick up a couple of bucks.

Related Jobs

Teacher assistants; teachers—kindergarten, elementary, middle, and secondary; teachers—preschool, except special education; teachers—special education

Education & Training
Short-term OJT

Earnings
$

Job Outlook
Average increase

Fitness Workers

On the Job

Fitness workers help people work out and get healthy. They teach proper exercise methods and lead exercise groups. Personal trainers work one-on-one with individuals to help them reach their fitness goals. Group exercise instructors, on the other hand, lead sessions of an activity like yoga or Pilates. Naturally these workers must be in good shape, although they are still prone to injury.

SOMETHING EXTRA

How much exercise is enough? Scientists, doctors, and researchers have debated this point, and the answers vary. But nearly all agree that a half hour of moderate physical activity a day is enough to keep your heart healthy and your energy up. Have you had your half hour of exercise today?

Subjects to Study

Physical education, biology, chemistry, psychology, dance

Discover More

Plan a weekly exercise routine for you and your family, making sure you get some kind of workout each day. The exercise could include indoor and outdoor activities, from doing a Wii workout to riding bikes to taking a walk. See whether you notice a difference in your energy and appearance after a few weeks of this routine.

Related Jobs

Athletes, coaches, umpires, and related workers; dietitians and nutritionists; physical therapists; recreation workers

Education & Training
Voc/tech training

Earnings
$$

Job Outlook
Rapid increase

Young Person's Occupational Outlook Handbook, © JIST Works

Flight Attendants

On the Job

Flight attendants help keep airline passengers safe and comfortable. In an emergency, they help passengers react calmly and quickly. They stock the plane with drinks, first-aid kits, and other supplies. During the flight, they serve drinks and answer questions. They may administer first aid to passengers who become ill. They work irregular hours, travel extensively, stay on their feet, and must remain calm in emergencies.

SOMETHING EXTRA

It used to be that all flight attendants were female—mostly young, unmarried women. Your flight attendant today is just as likely to be a man as a woman. They're not all young, either. While flight attendants must be physically fit and strong, many of the old requirements have gone the way of the dinosaurs. Mature women and men, working moms and dads, and people of all ethnic backgrounds are helping us fly today.

Subjects to Study

English, communication skills, foreign languages, speech, first aid, health, physical education

Discover More

For more information on becoming a flight attendant, visit the Web site for the Association of Flight Attendants: www.afanet.org.

Related Jobs

Emergency medical technicians and paramedics, fire fighters, food and beverage serving and related workers

Education & Training
Long-term OJT

Earnings
$$$

Job Outlook
Average increase

Gaming Services Occupations

On the Job

Most gaming services workers are employed by casinos—places where people play games of chance for money. Supervisors oversee the gaming tables and workers. Slot attendants watch over the slot machines, making sure everything is working smoothly. Gaming dealers operate games such as blackjack, craps, and roulette. All gaming workers must be licensed and have good customer-relations skills.

Subjects to Study

English, foreign languages, math, business courses, psychology

Discover More

You can learn the rules for different card and table games played in casinos, and about casino careers, by checking out www.americangaming. org. Or ask a parent or friend to teach you how to play.

Related Jobs

Cashiers, gaming cage workers, retail salespersons, sales worker supervisors, security guards and gaming surveillance officers

Education & Training
Voc/tech training

Earnings
$$$

Job Outlook
Declining

Recreation Workers

On the Job

Recreation workers are employed as camp counselors or coaches, organizing leisure activities at parks, health clubs, camps, tourist sites, and other places. They teach people how to use recreation equipment properly and safely. They often work nights and weekends. Recreation workers may be found in state and national parks, in health clubs, and on cruise ships. Many work part time.

Subjects to Study

English, communication skills, business courses, accounting, physical education, swimming, art, music, drama, sports

Discover More

Call your local YMCA, YWCA, Boys' or Girls' Club, or community center and volunteer to help out. You might be asked to watch younger children, teach them games, or help maintain equipment.

Related Jobs

Athletes, coaches, umpires, and related workers; counselors; fitness workers; probation officers and correctional treatment specialists; psychologists; recreational therapists; social workers; teachers—self enrichment education

Education & Training
Bachelor's degree

Earnings
$

Job Outlook
Above-average increase

Sales & Related Occupations

Advertising Sales Agents

On the Job

Advertising sales agents do exactly what the name suggests—they sell advertising, including space in publications and for Web sites, signs and billboards, and television and radio time. Some work with businesses to decide what forms of advertising will work best. Others work for media companies to sell the space they have for advertising. The work can be stressful because of irregular hours and sales quotas.

SOMETHING EXTRA

Advertising is everywhere. Ads are found on the Internet, the radio, and television; in magazines and newspapers; on billboards; on our shirts and shoes; in our schools; as part of our movie previews; and now as part of our bodies. That's right! Some advertisers pay individuals to wear temporary tattoos on their foreheads, pitching a product. People with long bangs need not apply.

Subjects to Study

Math, English, communication skills, computer skills, business courses, art, journalism, economics

Discover More

If your school has a newspaper, find out how you can get involved in its production. Contact businesses such as grocery stores and restaurants to see whether they would be willing to buy advertising space in your school paper.

Related Jobs

Advertising, marketing, promotions, public relations, and sales managers; insurance sales agents; real estate brokers and sales agents; sales engineers; sales representatives, wholesale and manufacturing; securities, commodities, and financial services sales agents

Education & Training
Moderate-term OJT

Earnings
$$$

Job Outlook
Average increase

Cashiers

On the Job

Cashiers add up customers' bills, take their money, and give change. They process credit and debit cards and give receipts. Cashiers are responsible for the money they collect during their shifts. They cannot leave their cash drawers without permission from their supervisor. Cashiers use cash registers, scanners, and computers regularly.

SOMETHING EXTRA

A cashier receives a specific amount of money in a cash drawer at the beginning of each work shift. The cashier counts this "bank" of money, for which he or she is responsible. At the end of the shift the cashier counts the bank again and compares the total to the sales information. Most employers understand if the drawer comes up short occasionally, but repeated shortages can get you fired.

Subjects to Study

Math, English, communication skills, computer skills, business courses

Discover More

Volunteer to work as a cashier at a church, club, or family rummage sale. Make sure you have enough money in the cash drawer to make change for the customers. Save the tags from the items paid for at your cash drawer. Add the total sales to the amount that was in your cash drawer before the sale. Then count the money in your drawer. Does it balance?

Related Jobs

Food and beverage serving and related workers, gaming cage workers, retail salespersons

Education & Training
Short-term OJT

Earnings
$

Job Outlook
Little change

Demonstrators & Product Promoters

On the Job

Demonstrators show products to customers in stores, malls, fairs, trade shows, or private homes. They must catch the attention of possible customers. They inform and educate customers about the features of products. Product promoters try to convince stores to carry new products. They may set up displays in stores or host special activities to show off their products. All of these workers travel as part of their jobs.

Subjects to Study

Communication skills, marketing, math, photography, speech, sociology, foreign languages, psychology

Discover More

Do a product demonstration for your class. Design a catchy poster and slogan, write a script, and come up with a gimmick to draw people's attention. Try to convince your classmates that they definitely want to have your product.

Related Jobs

Insurance sales agents; models; real estate brokers and sales agents; retail salespersons; sales representatives, wholesale and manufacturing

Education & Training
Moderate-term OJT

Earnings
$

Job Outlook
Average increase

Insurance Sales Agents

On the Job

Insurance agents sell insurance policies to people and businesses. Insurance policies protect the people and companies who buy them against different kinds of losses. Common policies include health, life, and car insurance. Insurance agents and brokers help people choose the policies that best meet their needs. Agents work for a single insurance company. Insurance brokers are independent and sell insurance for several different companies.

> ## SOMETHING EXTRA
>
> People buy insurance to protect their assets. But not all assets are cars or houses. The famous insurance group Lloyd's of London has issued some odd insurance policies. Some of these policies include accident insurance for Russian cosmonauts traveling to the MIR space station; coverage in case of a crocodile attack; and insuring a famous model's legs, a singer's vocal chords, and a food critic's taste buds.

Subjects to Study

Math, accounting, economics, government, psychology, sociology, speech, computer skills

Discover More

Ask your parents what kinds of insurance they have. How did they choose their insurance plans? Do they receive insurance through their employers?

Related Jobs

Advertising sales agents; claims adjusters, appraisers, examiners, and investigators; customer service representatives; financial analysts; financial managers; insurance underwriters; personal financial advisors; real estate brokers and sales agents; sales representatives, wholesale and manufacturing; securities, commodities, and financial services sales agents

Education & Training
Voc/tech training

Earnings
$$$$

Job Outlook
Average increase

Models

On the Job

Models create public interest in products such as clothing, cosmetics, food, and housewares. They pose for photos, paintings, or sculptures. Models appear in print publications, at live modeling events, and on television to promote products and services. During a photo shoot, a model poses to demonstrate the features of products. With the help of agents, models spend time promoting themselves and maintaining portfolios of their work.

SOMETHING EXTRA

Nearly everyone recognizes Tyra Banks, but how about Ellen Sirot? You might not know her name or face, but you might recognize her hands. They've been photographed holding everything from soft drinks to cell phones. She's a hand model. She makes a living showing off her slim wrists, tapering fingers, and healthy nails. If your hands aren't your best feature, how about something else? The modeling industry uses foot models, hair models, and even lip models. Your face may not be in Vogue, but your earlobes might!

Subjects to Study

Communication skills, marketing, photography, health, psychology

Discover More

Put on a hat or gloves and stand in front of a mirror. Change your expression, movements, and posture to make the hat or gloves something that other people will want to buy.

Related Jobs

Actors, producers, and directors; demonstrators and product promoters

Education & Training
Moderate-term OJT

Earnings
$$

Job Outlook
Above-average increase

Real Estate Brokers & Sales Agents

On the Job

Real estate agents and brokers help people buy and sell homes and rental properties. Real estate agents show homes, help buyers get financing, and make sure the contract conditions are met. Brokers may sell houses and rent and manage properties. These workers must know their local housing market. They must have a real estate license.

SOMETHING EXTRA

Location, location, location. It's the mantra of real estate, and it is reflected in the prices. The money you would spend on a one-bedroom apartment in San Diego could buy you a four-bedroom, two-story house in Toledo. A place on the water will cost more than one next to a noisy interstate highway. There's certainly no place like home.

Subjects to Study

Math, English, accounting, economics, business courses, communication skills, computer skills, psychology

Discover More

You can usually find free real estate and rental magazines at grocery stores or drugstores. Look through one to find out what homes and properties are available in your community. How much do homes and apartments in your area cost? Then flip through and see if you can find your dream house. How much does *it* cost?

Related Jobs

Appraisers and assessors of real estate; insurance sales agents; sales representatives, wholesale and manufacturing; securities, commodities, and financial services sales agents

Education & Training
Work experience to Voc/tech training

Earnings
$$$

Job Outlook
Above-average increase

Retail Salespersons

On the Job

Retail salespersons help customers choose and buy all kinds of items, from sweaters and makeup to lumber and plumbing. Their primary job is to interest customers in whatever products they are selling. They fill out sales checks, take payments, bag purchases, and give change and receipts. Most sales workers are responsible for keeping track of the money in their cash registers.

Subjects to Study

Math, English, communication skills, computer skills, psychology

Discover More

Watch the sales workers the next time you go shopping. What jobs do they do? How do they approach customers? How do they help you? Does their mood or approach affect your desire to buy their products?

Related Jobs

Cashiers; customer service representatives; gaming cage workers; insurance sales agents; real estate brokers and sales agents; sales engineers; sales representatives, wholesale and manufacturing; securities, commodities, and financial services sales agents

Education & Training
Short-term OJT

Earnings
$

Job Outlook
Average increase

Sales Engineers

On the Job

Sales engineers work for companies that produce complex products, such as chemicals or technical tools. They help customers decide which products or services will work best for them. Selling is an important part of the job, but sales engineers also help their customers learn to use the products they buy. They may help companies produce better materials based on customer feedback.

Subjects to Study

Math, chemistry, biology, physics, English, foreign languages, psychology

Discover More

For more information on becoming a sales engineer, contact the Manufacturers' Agents National Association at www.manaonline.org or the Manufacturers' Representatives Educational Research Foundation at www.mrerf.org.

Related Jobs

Advertising sales agents; engineers; insurance sales agents; purchasing managers, buyers, and purchasing agents; real estate brokers and sales agents; retail salespersons; sales representatives, wholesale and manufacturing; sales worker supervisors; securities, commodities, and financial services sales agents

Education & Training
Bachelor's degree

Earnings
$$$$$

Job Outlook
Average increase

Sales Representatives, Wholesale & Manufacturing

On the Job

Manufacturing and whole-sale sales representatives sell products to businesses, government agencies, and other institutions, often traveling for several days or weeks at a time. They answer questions about their products and show clients how the products can meet their needs and save them money. They take orders and resolve problems or complaints about their merchandise.

SOMETHING EXTRA

Most sales representatives are paid on commission. Instead of receiving a regular paycheck, they get paid based on their sales: The more they sell, the more money they make. Few or no sales mean little or no money. Many sales mean big paychecks. Salespeople must learn to budget and pay their bills knowing that their income is unpredictable.

Subjects to Study

Math, English, speech, communication skills, accounting, business courses, psychology, foreign languages, computer skills, marketing

Discover More

Think of some businesses in your community (such as hospitals, grocery stores, and restaurants) that might order products from manufacturers' sales representatives. What kind of products would each of these businesses buy?

Related Jobs

Advertising sales agents; insurance sales agents; purchasing managers, buyers, and purchasing agents; real estate brokers and sales agents; retail salespersons; sales engineers; sales worker supervisors; securities, commodities, and financial services sales agents

Education & Training
Work experience

Earnings
$$$$

Job Outlook
Average increase

Young Person's Occupational Outlook Handbook, © JIST Works

Sales Worker Supervisors

On the Job

Sales worker supervisors can be found in all kinds of stores—clothing shops, home improvement stores, grocery stores, department stores, and bakeries, to name a few. They hire, train, and supervise workers. They schedule workers. They order supplies, keep the books, make bank deposits, and often wait on customers. Most work evenings and weekends, and they spend a lot of time on their feet.

SOMETHING EXTRA

Many people in our economy work standard hours—8 a.m. to 5 p.m., Monday through Friday. They like having evenings and weekends free and knowing exactly when they will work. But other people thrive on different hours. Maybe you're a night person who enjoys working evenings. Maybe you prefer working on a Saturday and taking a day off in the middle of the week so that you can hit the beach when it's not crowded. Retail managers often work nights and weekends but have time off during the week.

Subjects to Study

Math, English, psychology, business courses, communication skills, computer skills

Discover More

Visit a shop in your neighborhood and ask the manager if you can help out after school one or two days a week. You might stock shelves or clean up. Watch the manager at work and ask about the best and worst parts of the job.

Related Jobs

Administrative services managers; advertising, marketing, promotions, public relations, and sales managers; food service managers; lodging managers; office and administrative support worker supervisors and managers

Education & Training
Work experience

Earnings
$$$

Job Outlook
Little change

Securities, Commodities & Financial Services Sales Agents

On the Job

Securities and commodities sales agents buy and sell stocks, bonds, and other financial products for clients who want to invest in the stock market. They explain terms and the advantages and disadvantages of different investments. Financial service sales agents usually work for banks. They contact potential customers to sell their bank's services, which might include retirement planning and other investment services.

> ### SOMETHING EXTRA
>
> Charles Dow published the first daily newspaper that gave financial information about companies. That paper grew into the *Wall Street Journal*. Dow also developed the first stock market average, which became known as the Dow Jones Industrial Average. Interestingly, he never finished high school (although you definitely should).

Subjects to Study

Math, English, communication skills, computer skills, speech, accounting, economics, psychology, government, business courses

Discover More

Find stock market listings online. Ask a parent or teacher to explain them to you. Listen to the stock market report on news programs. Look up some individual stocks on the Internet.

Related Jobs

Financial analysts, insurance sales agents, loan officers, personal financial advisors, real estate brokers and sales agents

Education & Training
Bachelor's degree

Earnings
$$$$$

Job Outlook
Average increase

Travel Agents

On the Job

Travel agents make hotel, airline, car-rental, and cruise reservations for people and businesses. They plan group tours and conferences. They tell clients what papers are needed to travel in foreign countries. They must be up-to-date on cultural and political issues, restaurants, and tourist attractions.

SOMETHING EXTRA

While many travel agents plan getaways to the Bahamas or family cruises, some specialize in more unusual destinations. Whether it's planning a climb up Mount Kilimanjaro or tracking gorillas through the Bwindi Impenetrable Forest, agents can plan that exotic trip for you. Though it probably wouldn't be cheap, it would certainly be memorable.

Subjects to Study

Communication skills, computer skills, geography, English, foreign languages, history, math, business courses

Discover More

What foreign country are you curious about? Read about that country and find it on a map. Then find an Internet site where you can learn more about life in that country. Finally, make a list of all the places you would like to visit in your lifetime.

Related Jobs

Reservation and transportation ticket agents and travel clerks

Education & Training
Voc/tech training

Earnings
$$

Job Outlook
Declining

Office & Administrative Support Occupations

Bill & Account Collectors

On the Job

Bill and account collectors keep track of accounts that are overdue and try to collect payment on them. Some are employed by collection agencies; others work directly for companies such as stores, hospitals, or banks. They use computers and special software to keep track of clients. They spend a lot of time on the phone. Because money can be a sensitive matter, collectors must have good people skills while still being persistent.

Subjects to Study

Math, English, computer skills, business courses, accounting, psychology, foreign languages

Discover More

Spend half a day in the collection office of your local hospital. Talk to the collectors and ask about their most interesting cases. Many have wild stories about people going to great lengths to escape paying their bills.

Related Jobs

Credit authorizers, checkers, and clerks; customer service representatives; interviewers, except eligibility and loan; loan officers; sales representatives, wholesale and manufacturing

Education & Training
Short-term OJT

Earnings
$$

Job Outlook
Above-average increase

Bookkeeping, Accounting & Auditing Clerks

On the Job

Bookkeeping and accounting clerks keep records of all the money their company spends and receives. They prepare reports, post bank deposits, and pay bills. Auditing clerks check the financial records of other employees in an organization and correct errors they find. These clerks must be careful in their work to ensure the accuracy of financial records. They must be comfortable using computers.

SOMETHING EXTRA

Businesses must keep track of how they spend their money. Otherwise, they might go out of business. Accurate bookkeepers are crucial to a company's success. Knowing how money is being spent helps managers make good decisions that benefit all of the company's employees. In case of a tax audit, accurate financial records can keep the business out of trouble with the IRS!

Subjects to Study

Math, office skills, computer skills, English, business courses, accounting

Discover More

Keep your own financial records. Use a notebook to record any money you receive from allowance, gifts, or chores. Then record how you spend your money. Keep your receipts and banking records in a file.

Related Jobs

Accountants and auditors

Education & Training
Moderate-term OJT

Earnings
$$$

Job Outlook
Average increase

Gaming Cage Workers

On the Job

Gaming cage workers, also called cage cashiers, work in casinos and other gaming companies. The "cage" they work in is the central depository for money, chips, and paperwork. They do credit checks on people who want to open a casino credit account and sell gambling chips, tokens, and tickets. They use cash registers and computers to add up transactions. They must follow strict rules and regulations when handling money.

Subjects to Study

Math, business courses, English, foreign languages

Discover More

To learn about careers in the gaming industry, check out the Web site for the American Gaming Association: www.americangaming.org.

Related Jobs

Cashiers, gaming service occupations, retail salespersons, sales worker supervisors

Education & Training
Short-term OJT

Earnings
$

Job Outlook
Declining

Customer Service Representatives

On the Job

Customer service representatives work directly with customers, answering questions, taking orders, and solving problems. Many work for utilities, such as electric or gas companies. They may handle billing mistakes, arrange for customers to have services switched on or off, and listen to complaints. These workers spend a lot of time on the phone. The work can be repetitious and stressful.

Subjects to Study

English, foreign languages, psychology, office skills, computer skills

Discover More

The next time you have a problem with a product or service, pay special attention to how the customer service representative handles it. He or she must stay calm under pressure, be polite and helpful, and work quickly and efficiently. That's provided you get around to talking to a human being, of course.

Related Jobs

Bill and account collectors; computer support specialists; insurance sales agents; retail salespersons; securities, commodities, and financial services sales agents

Education & Training
Moderate-term OJT

Earnings
$$

Job Outlook
Above-average increase

Receptionists & Information Clerks

On the Job

Receptionists greet customers on the phone and in person and refer them to the proper person or department. Making a good first impression is an important part of this job, because the receptionist is the first person most customers or clients meet. Some receptionists are responsible for coordinating incoming and outgoing mail. Information clerks file papers, make copies, do basic data entry, and may also be asked to answer phones.

SOMETHING EXTRA

Receptionists know who belongs where in an organization. Because of this, they are an important part of the security system at most companies. In larger companies, receptionists might give visitors identification cards or ask someone to escort a visitor to the proper office. They often are the first to meet visitors and the first to spot problems or suspicious characters.

Subjects to Study

English, communication skills, speech, computer skills, psychology, foreign languages, business courses, office skills

Discover More

Volunteer to be a greeter or an usher for a school play, a sports event, or a dance. Help people with their questions and concerns. Do you enjoy working with the public?

Related Jobs

Customer service representatives; secretaries and administrative assistants

Education & Training
Short-term OJT

Earnings
$$

Job Outlook
Above-average increase

Cargo & Freight Agents

On the Job

Cargo and freight agents sort cargo according to its destination, determine shipping rates and other costs, and then track the shipments. They take orders from customers and arrange for pickup of items for delivery to loading platforms. They check on missing or damaged items. Cargo and freight agents work for air and railroad carriers, trucking services, businesses, and stores. Some work in warehouses and outside on loading platforms.

SOMETHING EXTRA

Do you love to travel? Do you want to visit faraway, exotic places? If so, being a freight agent with an airline might be the job for you. Many air carriers have overseas offices where American employees work. And many airlines offer their employees free travel on their planes. Of course, you'll have to fly standby, but it's the best frequent-flyer deal you'll find.

Subjects to Study

Math, English, foreign languages, business courses, bookkeeping, geography

Discover More

Call a freight service in your town and ask if you can spend a day shadowing a freight agent. Pay attention to the kinds of tasks he or she performs. Ask about the best and worst aspects of the job.

Related Jobs

Shipping, receiving, and traffic clerks

Education & Training
Moderate-term OJT

Earnings
$$$

Job Outlook
Rapid increase

Couriers & Messengers

On the Job

Messengers and couriers drive, walk, or ride bicycles to pick up and deliver letters and packages that must be delivered quickly—usually within a city and the surrounding area. Most work for courier services. Many others are self-employed and provide their own vehicles. Some messengers are paid by how many deliveries they make and how far they travel.

SOMETHING EXTRA

Have you always wanted to run your own business and be your own boss? If so, courier and messenger services might be perfect for you. Many of these workers are self-employed. All it takes is reliable transportation and a cell phone. You'll spend your days moving from place to place. When you're ready to close shop, simply turn off the phone! Just beware of bad weather—and mean dogs.

Subjects to Study

English, foreign languages, driver's education, geography

Discover More

Start your own local courier service. Offer to deliver packages at your school, church, or local hospital. You will pick up your packages at the main office and deliver them to other rooms in the building, or perhaps to other buildings.

Related Jobs

Cargo and freight agents; Postal Service mail carriers; shipping, receiving, and traffic clerks; truck drivers and driver/sales workers

Education & Training
Short-term OJT

Earnings
$

Job Outlook
Declining

Postal Service Mail Carriers

On the Job

Mail carriers deliver billions of pieces of mail each week to homes and businesses. They travel on foot or by car in all kinds of weather. They also pick up mail from homes and businesses on their route. Mail carriers start work at the post office early in the morning, when they arrange the mail in delivery sequence. Automated equipment has reduced the time that carriers need to sort the mail.

SOMETHING EXTRA

Stamps with errors in printing or design are often more valuable than the number printed on them—and gain value as they get older. Take the world's most expensive stamp—a Swedish one that was printed in yellow-orange instead of green. It was discovered by a 14-year-old boy in 1885. It recently sold for more than $2 million dollars! Imagine finding that in your mailbox.

Subjects to Study

English, physical education, driver's education, communication skills, computer skills

Discover More

Find out who delivers your mail and talk to your carrier about his or her job. Does your carrier walk or drive? What are the working hours? What does your carrier like or dislike about the job?

Related Jobs

Couriers and messengers, truck drivers and driver/sales workers

Education & Training
Short-term OJT

Earnings
$$$$

Job Outlook
Declining

Shipping, Receiving & Traffic Clerks

On the Job

Traffic clerks keep records of all freight coming in and leaving a company and make sure the company is charged correctly. Shipping clerks keep records on all outgoing shipments. They fill orders from the stockroom and direct workers who load products onto trucks. Receiving clerks check materials coming into the warehouse, make sure they are in good condition, and send them to the right departments.

SOMETHING EXTRA

Technology has changed the way warehouses operate. Many warehouse workers use handheld computer scanners, which help them check in goods more quickly. Some warehouses have conveyer belts run by computers and robots that move materials faster than people can move them. Gone are the days of the pencil and clipboard.

Subjects to Study

Math, computer skills, business courses, bookkeeping

Discover More

Make a list of basic items you use every day, such as toothpaste, tissues, soap, and shampoo. Or make a list of the supplies you use at school. Check your personal inventory. What items do you need to restock?

Related Jobs

Cargo and freight agents, material moving occupations

Education & Training
Short-term OJT

Earnings
$$

Job Outlook
Declining

Desktop Publishers

On the Job

Desktop publishers use computers and software to format text, photos, charts, and other graphic elements to produce newsletters, magazines, calendars, business cards, newspapers, books, and other publications. Most work in firms that handle commercial printing and in newspaper plants, but many are self-employed.

SOMETHING EXTRA

Publishing has changed drastically in the last three decades. In the past, printers used the hot type method to print materials. Molten lead created individual letters, paragraphs, and full pages of text. Making changes to a page was very difficult once the type was set. Today, the hot type method has gone the way of the dodo. Sitting at a computer, you can produce publications and make changes easily and quickly. You'll never go near molten lead!

Subjects to Study

Computer skills, office skills, art, graphic design, photography, English, business courses

Discover More

Use a personal computer at home or school to design your own newsletter, or volunteer to work on your school newspaper or yearbook. Look through several magazines and newsletters—what catches your eye? What would you change? Can you think of a more attractive way to present the material?

Related Jobs

Artists and related workers, commercial and industrial designers, graphic designers, prepress technicians and workers

Education & Training
Short-term OJT

Earnings
$$

Job Outlook
Above-average increase

Office Clerks, General

On the Job

General office clerks work in all kinds of businesses, from doctors' offices to banks, from big law firms to small companies. Because a business's needs change from day to day, a clerk's job duties do, too. These workers file, do word processing, keep records, prepare mailings, and proofread documents for mistakes. Senior clerks may be responsible for supervising other workers.

Subjects to Study

English, word processing, computer skills, math, office skills, bookkeeping, accounting, business courses

Discover More

Can you type? Typing well is important in this and almost any other job. Many offices require clerks to type at least 60 words per minute. Take a word-processing class, practice, and become a good typist.

Related Jobs

Bookkeeping, accounting, and auditing clerks; customer service representatives; receptionists and information clerks; secretaries and administrative assistants

Education & Training
Short-term OJT

Earnings
$$

Job Outlook
Average increase

Secretaries & Administrative Assistants

On the Job

Secretaries and administrative assistants keep offices organized and running smoothly. They schedule appointments, maintain files, handle correspondence, greet visitors, and answer telephone calls. They work with office equipment such as computers, fax machines, and copiers. They may supervise clerks and other office workers. Some, such as medical and legal secretaries, do highly specialized work.

SOMETHING EXTRA

In the past, people thought of secretaries as low-level staff—young women who typed, answered phones, and made coffee. Today's reality is much different. A secretary or administrative assistant now is a kind of junior executive, the keeper of the office schedules and key information. Men and women working as administrative assistants often have access to confidential information and the company credit card. Most businesspeople know that a company is only as good as its administrative assistants.

Subjects to Study

English, spelling and grammar, speech, computer skills, office skills, math

Discover More

Talk to the secretaries at your school about their training and job duties. Develop some office skills, such as filing and word processing.

Related Jobs

Bookkeeping, accounting, and auditing clerks; court reporters; medical assistants; medical records and health information technicians; paralegals and legal assistants; receptionists and information clerks

Education & Training
Moderate-term OJT to Associate degree

Earnings
$$$

Job Outlook
Average increase

Farming, Fishing & Forestry Occupations

Fishers & Fishing Vessel Operators

On the Job

Fishers and fishing vessel operators catch and trap fish and seafood for restaurants and grocery stores. The boat's captain oversees the fishing, hires crew members, and arranges for the day's catch to be sold. The first mate is the captain's assistant and is in charge when the captain is not on duty. The boatswain helps the captain oversee the deckhands, who carry out the sailing and fishing operations. These workers may spend weeks or months at sea. The work is hard and sometimes dangerous, and employment can be seasonal.

SOMETHING EXTRA

Moby-Dick, Herman Melville's classic book, tells the story of a sea captain's obsessive battle with a particularly vindictive white whale. Ahab and his crew spend months chasing the huge beast. The final epic battle takes the captain's life. These days, whale-hunting is illegal for all but a few Native American groups. But sailors on fishing vessels still spend months on the ocean, battling fatigue and the elements—though few of them, if any, have wooden legs.

Subjects to Study

Physical education, shop courses, navigation, math, first aid

Discover More

Take a boating-safety course to learn more about sailing. To find one near you, check out BoatSafe Kids at www.boatsafe.com/kids/index.htm, which has information on classes, online courses, books, activities, and other Web sites.

Related Jobs

Water transportation occupations

Education & Training
Moderate-term OJT

Earnings
$$

Job Outlook
Declining

Forest & Conservation Workers

On the Job

Forest and conservation workers help develop and protect forests by planting new trees, fighting the pests and diseases that attack trees, and controlling soil erosion. They maintain forest facilities, such as roads and campsites. Some work in forest nurseries or tree farms. These workers are outdoors in all kinds of weather.

Subjects to Study

Physical education, first aid, shop courses, botany, biology

Discover More

Learn to identify the different trees in your area. Study a tree identification book and then visit a forest or park. How many trees can you identify?

Related Jobs

Conservation scientists and foresters, grounds maintenance workers, material moving operators

Education & Training
Moderate-term OJT

Earnings
$

Job Outlook
Average increase

Logging Workers

On the Job

Logging workers cut down thousands of acres of forests each year for the timber that is used for wood and paper products. The timber-cutting and logging process is carried out by a logging crew. Crew members use equipment to harvest the trees, cut logs, drag cut trees to the loading deck, and load the logs onto trucks. Although the operation has become more mechanized, the work is demanding and dangerous.

SOMETHING EXTRA

Sometimes a job has its own language. For example, if you spent time with logging workers, you would hear different job titles. Fallers and buckers cut down trees. Choker setters fasten chokers (steel chains) around logs to be skidded (dragged) by tractors to the landing. Riggers set up and dismantle the cables and guide wires on the logs.

Subjects to Study

Physical education, first aid, shop courses, biology

Discover More

Do you recycle paper at home and at school? Learn how paper gets recycled and how to increase your recycling. Visit www.paperrecycles.org/school_recycling/index.html.

Related Jobs

Conservation scientists and foresters, construction equipment operators, forest and conservation workers, grounds maintenance workers, material moving occupations

Education & Training
Moderate-term OJT

Earnings
$$

Job Outlook
Little change

Agricultural Workers, Other

On the Job

Agricultural workers play a large role in getting food and plants to us. They plant, grade, and sort farm products. They work with food crops, animals, trees, and plants. They may work indoors or outdoors, in all kinds of conditions. They may work long, irregular hours. Many agricultural worker jobs are seasonal, so some workers do other jobs during slow times.

Subjects to Study

Physical education, shop courses, driver's education, biology, botany

Discover More

Plant a garden in your yard or at a community plot. Try your hand at growing some food items: Broccoli, peppers, and tomatoes are easy starters. Look for nonchemical ways to control bugs and other pests. When your crop is ready, make a salad and treat your family to dinner.

Related Jobs

Animal care and service workers, fishers and fishing vessel operators, forest and conservation workers, grounds maintenance workers, veterinarians, veterinary technologists and technicians

Education & Training
Work experience

Earnings
$

Job Outlook
Little change

Construction Trades & Related Workers

Boilermakers

On the Job

Boilermakers build boilers, vats, and other large tanks used for storing liquids and gases. Boilers supply steam for electric engines and for heating and power systems in buildings, factories, and ships. Because most boilers last for 35 years or more, repairing and maintaining them is a big part of a boilermaker's job. These workers use dangerous equipment, lift heavy items, and may work on ladders or scaffolding.

Subjects to Study

Math, shop courses, blueprint reading, welding

Discover More

Most boilermakers belong to labor unions. Find out which labor unions are active in your community. Contact one and ask about what the union does and how people become members. Or visit the International Brotherhood of Boilermakers' Web site at www.boilermakers.org.

Related Jobs

Assemblers and fabricators; industrial machinery mechanics and millwrights; machinists; plumbers, pipelayers, pipefitters, and steamfitters; sheet metal workers; tool and die makers; welding, soldering, and brazing workers

Education & Training
Long-term OJT

Earnings
$$$$

Job Outlook
Above-average increase

Brickmasons, Blockmasons & Stonemasons

On the Job

These workers lay sidewalks and patios, build fireplaces, and install ornamental exteriors on buildings. Brickmasons work with firebrick linings in furnaces and with bricks. Blockmasons work with concrete blocks. Stonemasons work with natural and artificial stones. They build walls on churches, office buildings, and hotels. These workers are outdoors in all types of weather. They must be strong enough to move heavy materials. Many are self-employed.

SOMETHING EXTRA

You may have heard of Boy Scout Camp and church camp, but have you heard of Masonry Camp? Each year, the International Masonry Institute sponsors a Masonry Camp on Swan's Island in Maine. For one week, architects, engineers, and masonry apprentices work together to design and build a challenging project. This way, workers from several fields learn how building plans translate from paper to bricks and mortar.

Subjects to Study

Math, mechanical drawing, shop courses, art, physical education

Discover More

You can learn more about brick and stonework training programs by checking out the International Masonry Institute's Web site at www.imiweb.org.

Related Jobs

Carpenters; carpet, floor, and tile installers and finishers; cement masons, concrete finishers, segmental pavers, and terrazzo workers; drywall and ceiling tile installers, tapers, plasterers, and stucco masons

Education & Training
Long-term OJT

Earnings
$$$

Job Outlook
Average increase

Carpenters

On the Job

Carpenters do all kinds of construction work, including woodworking, concrete work, drywall work, and many other jobs. They replace doors, windows, and locks; repair wooden furniture; hang kitchen cabinets; and install machinery. They work with hand and power tools and read blueprints. Most work in new construction or remodeling. Others are self-employed.

Subjects to Study

Shop courses, mechanical drawing, carpentry, math

Discover More

Try a simple carpentry project, such as building a doghouse, a shelf, or a flower box. First, get a plan and gather the materials you need. Be sure you know how to use your tools safely before you begin.

Related Jobs

Brickmasons, blockmasons, and stonemasons; cement masons, concrete finishers, segmental pavers, and terrazzo workers; construction equipment operators; drywall and ceiling tile installers, tapers, plasterers, and stucco masons; electricians; plumbers, pipelayers, pipefitters, and steamfitters

Education & Training
Long-term OJT

Earnings
$$$

Job Outlook
Average increase

Carpet, Floor & Tile Installers & Finishers

On the Job

Carpet installers put carpet in buildings and houses. Floor layers install flooring foundation materials such as rubber and linoleum, which act as sound dampers. Tilesetters use grout to apply ceramic tiles to floors and walls. All of these installers work regular daytime hours, but some work evenings as well. These workers spend their days kneeling, bending, stretching, and lifting heavy rolls of carpet and other materials.

Subjects to Study

Shop courses, physical education, math, art

Discover More

Carpet installers must measure rooms precisely. Using a tape measure and a calculator, measure a room in your house. Include nooks, bends, and closets. Take the total width of the room and multiply by the total length to get the square footage.

Related Jobs

Brickmasons, blockmasons, and stonemasons; carpenters; cement masons, concrete finishers, segmental pavers, and terrazzo workers; drywall and ceiling tile installers, tapers, plasterers, and stucco masons; painters and paperhangers; roofers; sheet metal workers

Education & Training
Moderate-term OJT to Long-term OJT

Earnings
$$$

Job Outlook
Average increase

Cement Masons, Concrete Finishers, Segmental Pavers & Terrazzo Workers

On the Job

Cement masons and concrete finishers use a mixture of cement, gravel, sand, and water to build home patios, huge dams, and miles of roads. They pour the concrete and smooth the surface. Segmental pavers lay out flat pieces of masonry to form paths, patios, playgrounds, and driveways. Terrazzo workers add marble chips to the surface of concrete to create decorative walls and sidewalks. These workers spend their days outdoors, bending, stooping, and kneeling. Most wear kneepads and water-repellent boots.

SOMETHING EXTRA

Have you heard the expression "All roads lead to Rome"? The ancient Romans took their road building seriously. Only Roman men of the highest rank were allowed to build and maintain the roads. At the height of the Roman Empire, 29 different roads led from Rome to the farthest stretches of the empire, to Northern Europe and the Middle East, and even into parts of Africa. Those cement-block roads were so well constructed that they have lasted for more than 2,000 years.

Subjects to Study

Shop courses, blueprint reading, mechanical drawing, physical education, math

Discover More

Most crafts stores offer decorative concrete molds for making your own stepping stones. These kits require you to mix concrete, make imprints, and place decorative tiles. Ask a parent to help you make one.

Related Jobs

Brickmasons, blockmasons, and stonemasons; carpet, floor, and tile installers and finishers; drywall and ceiling tile installers, tapers, plasterers, and stucco masons

Education & Training
Moderate-term OJT to Long-term OJT

Earnings
$$$

Job Outlook
Average increase

Construction & Building Inspectors

On the Job

Construction and building inspectors make sure that the country's buildings, roads, sewers, dams, and bridges are safe. They may check electrical or plumbing systems, elevators, or the beams and girders on skyscrapers. They climb high ladders, crawl through underground tunnels, and squeeze into tight spaces to do their jobs.

SOMETHING EXTRA

In 1989, a magnitude-6.8 earthquake hit Armenia in Central Asia. Thousands of buildings collapsed, killing more than 25,000 people. A year later, San Francisco was hit with an even larger earthquake, and 62 people died. Why the difference in fatalities? Buildings, roads, and bridges in California must meet strict building codes. Those codes and the inspectors who enforce them saved thousands of lives.

Subjects to Study

Math, geometry, algebra, drafting, shop courses, computer skills

Discover More

Inspectors often use photographs in their reports. Practice your photography skills by taking pictures of building details in your neighborhood. Do you see anything that might be unsafe?

Related Jobs

Appraisers and assessors of real estate; architects, except landscape and naval; carpenters; construction managers; cost estimators; electricians; engineering technicians; engineers; plumbers, pipelayers, pipefitters, and steamfitters; surveyors, cartographers, photogrammetrists, and surveying and mapping technicians

Education & Training
Work experience

Earnings
$$$$

Job Outlook
Above-average increase

Construction Equipment Operators

On the Job

Construction equipment operators run the huge machinery used in constructing roads and buildings and in demolition. They might operate cranes, tractors, scrapers, backhoes, pavers, cement mixers, tamping machines, or hoists. They work outdoors in every kind of weather at construction sites, shipping docks, airports, mines, and on highways. The pay can be high, but the work may slow down in bad weather, reducing earnings. The work schedule can be erratic and require late night and early morning shifts.

SOMETHING EXTRA

We've all seen Fred Flintstone sliding down the back of his Brontosaurus crane yelling "yabba-dabba-do!" Does it look like fun? Well, consider this: The largest dinosaur that scientists have identified is the Memenchisaurus, which towered 75 feet above the ground—roughly the height of a four-story building. Still think you're up for the ride? Consider first that tower crane operators today routinely sit in a cab 275 feet off the ground! At least it's more comfortable than sitting on top of a dinosaur's head.

Subjects to Study

Electronics, shop courses, science, physical education

Discover More

To learn more about jobs operating these huge machines, check out the Web site of the International Union of Operating Engineers, which offers apprenticeships and training programs: www.iuoe.org.

Related Jobs

Material moving occupations

Education & Training
Moderate-term OJT

Earnings
$$$

Job Outlook
Average increase

Construction Laborers

On the Job

Construction laborers do a wide range of physically demanding jobs. They build skyscrapers and houses, roads, and mine shafts. They remove waste materials and tear down buildings. The work can be dangerous when they work at great heights, remove hazardous chemicals, or work underground. Some work only during the warmer months.

SOMETHING EXTRA

Who built the great pyramids of Egypt? If you answer the pharaohs, you are mistaken. The pharaohs funded the pyramids, but it was construction laborers who did the actual building. Using only the technology of ancient times, these workers cut huge stones from quarries, shaped them into building blocks, moved them from the quarries to the building sites, and then raised them hundreds of feet, layer upon layer. It's a spectacular feat, even by modern standards.

Subjects to Study

Shop courses, physical education, driver's education

Discover More

Offer your services to your family or neighbors the next time they are planning a construction project. You might help build a porch or deck, pave a driveway, or haul materials to and from the worksite.

Related Jobs

Assemblers and fabricators; brickmasons, blockmasons, and stonemasons; forest and conservation workers; grounds maintenance workers; logging workers; material moving occupations

Education & Training
Moderate-term OJT

Earnings
$$

Job Outlook
Rapid increase

Drywall & Ceiling Tile Installers, Tapers, Plasterers & Stucco Masons

On the Job

These specialty construction workers build, apply, or fasten wallboards or wall coverings to homes and other structures. Drywall and ceiling tile installers and tapers work indoors, installing wallboards to ceilings or to walls. Plasterers and stucco masons work indoors and outdoors, applying plaster to inside walls and cement or stucco to outside walls. Some work is decorative. These workers spend their days standing, reaching, and bending. They work on ladders, high scaffolding, and stilts.

Subjects to Study

Shop courses, carpentry, blueprint reading, mechanical drawing, art, physical education, math

Discover More

Visit a home improvement store and look at the drywall pieces. Ask the sales workers how the boards are cut and what tools drywall workers use.

Related Jobs

Brickmasons, blockmasons, and stonemasons; carpenters; carpet, floor, and tile installers and finishers; cement masons, concrete finishers, segmental pavers, and terrazzo workers; insulation workers

Education & Training
Moderate-term OJT to Long-term OJT

Earnings
$$$

Job Outlook
Average increase

Electricians

On the Job

Electricians work with the systems that provide electricity to homes, businesses, and factories. They may install and repair wiring, heating, and air-conditioning systems. They must follow government rules and building codes for safety. Electricians may work nights and weekends and be on call 24 hours a day. Many are self-employed.

SOMETHING EXTRA

Benjamin Franklin contributed a great deal to our understanding of electricity, including naming the electrical charges (positive and negative) and helping to prove that lightning was a form of electricity. You may have seen drawings of Franklin flying a kite in a lightning storm, trying to harness electricity. While it is true that he performed this experiment, Franklin was not in the conducting path, because he probably would have been electrocuted.

Subjects to Study

Math, shop courses, electronics, mechanical drawing, science, blueprint reading

Discover More

Can you get power from a lemon? Try this experiment using a strip of copper, a strip of zinc, a small flashlight bulb, and a lemon. Insert the metal strips into the lemon, close together but not touching. Now put the end of the light bulb on the zinc and the end of the copper on the threads. The acid in the lemon should make the bulb light up.

Related Jobs

Computer, automated teller, and office machine repairers; electrical and electronics installers and repairers; electronic home entertainment equipment installers and repairers; elevator installers and repairers; heating, air-conditioning, and refrigeration mechanics and installers; line installers and repairers

Education & Training
Long-term OJT

Earnings
$$$$

Job Outlook
Average increase

Elevator Installers & Repairers

On the Job

Elevator installers and repairers assemble, install, fix, and replace elevators, escalators, chairlifts, dumbwaiters, and moving walkways. They test the equipment to make sure it works properly. These workers must have a thorough knowledge of electricity and electronics. They may be on call 24 hours a day to help in an emergency.

SOMETHING EXTRA

You might think that the elevator is a modern invention. But people have been using lifting devices since the 13th century. These early devices were powered by people or animals. It wasn't until the late 1800s that the modern elevator made its debut. This machine, powered by electricity, made skyscrapers possible. Imagine trying to climb stairs to the top of the Willis Tower every day to go to work!

Subjects to Study

Math, shop courses, science courses, electronics, physics

Discover More

Learn about apprenticeship programs by visiting the Web site of the International Union of Elevator Constructors at www.iuec.org.

Related Jobs

Boilermakers, electrical and electronics installers and repairers, electricians, industrial machinery mechanics and millwrights, sheet metal workers, structural and reinforcing iron and metal workers

Education & Training
Long-term OJT

Earnings
$$$$$

Job Outlook
Average increase

Glaziers

On the Job

Glaziers cut, install, and remove all kinds of glass and plastics in doors, windows, showers, and baths. They often use glass that is precut and mounted in a frame. They may use cranes to lift large, heavy pieces into place. Once the glass is mounted, glaziers secure it with bolts, cement, metal clips, or wood molding. Glaziers work outdoors in all kinds of weather. They sometimes work on ladders and high scaffolding.

SOMETHING EXTRA

You've probably seen stained glass, but do you know how it's made? Most stained glass today is clear glass that's been painted with silver oxide or pot-metal glass that's been colored in its molten state. The earliest colored glass we know about is from 306 B.C., when builders in the Far East used it for windows in homes and public buildings.

Subjects to Study

Shop courses, math, blueprint reading, mechanical drawing

Discover More

Make your own stained-glass creation by getting a window-hanger kit from your local craft store. These kits contain metal frames and small, colored beads. You fill the frame with beads and then put it in the oven to melt the beads so that they look like glass.

Related Jobs

Automotive body and related repairers; brickmasons, blockmasons, and stonemasons; carpenters; carpet, floor, and tile installers and finishers; cement masons, concrete finishers, segmental pavers, and terrazzo workers; painters and paperhangers; sheet metal workers

Education & Training
Long-term OJT

Earnings
$$$

Job Outlook
Average increase

Hazardous Materials Removal Workers

On the Job

These workers identify, remove, package, transport, and dispose of materials that are dangerous to human beings. They might deal with asbestos, lead, or radioactive materials. They wear protective clothing, including coveralls, gloves, shoe covers, face shields, and respirators. They must follow strict safety guidelines, and the work may require climbing or crawling into tight spaces. They may work overtime to meet deadlines or handle emergencies.

SOMETHING EXTRA

Did you know that, until the 1970s, lead was a common ingredient in house paint? Then researchers began proving that lead is toxic to humans—especially children. For years, people scraping old paint from their walls and windowsills had been releasing lead-filled dust into their homes and slowly poisoning their kids. Lead poisoning can lead to learning disabilities and lower IQs in children.

Subjects to Study

Math, chemistry, biology, physical education

Discover More

Do you know what kinds of hazardous materials are in your community? To find out, check out Environmental Defense's Scorecard at www. scorecard.org. Just type in your ZIP code and you'll get a complete list of pollutants that are being released into the environment near you and who is releasing them.

Related Jobs

Fire fighters; insulation workers; painters and paperhangers; police and detectives; power plant operators, distributors, and dispatchers; sheet metal workers; water and liquid waste treatment plant and system operators

Education & Training
Moderate-term OJT

Earnings
$$$

Job Outlook
Above-average increase

Insulation Workers

On the Job

Builders put insulation in buildings to save energy by keeping the heat in during the winter and the heat out during the summer. Insulation workers cement, staple, wire, tape, or spray insulation between the inner and outer walls or under the roof of a building. They often use a hose or blowing machine to spray a liquid insulation that dries into place. These workers must wear protective suits, masks, and respirators. Many are self-employed.

SOMETHING EXTRA

Have you heard of asbestos? It's a material that was once widely used for insulation in homes and buildings. It is fire-resistant and very effective. Unfortunately, it also causes cancer in people exposed to it. Insulation workers who deal with asbestos must wear protective clothing, gloves, and masks to prevent asbestos contamination.

Subjects to Study

Shop courses, blueprint reading, physical education

Discover More

Head to a home improvement store and check out the different kinds of insulation. Ask the sales worker about each kind. Ask your parents what kind of insulation your home has. If you live in an apartment building, ask the building manager.

Related Jobs

Carpenters; carpet, floor, and tile installers and finishers; drywall and ceiling tile installers, tapers, plasterers, and stucco masons; roofers; sheet metal workers

Education & Training
Moderate-term OJT

Earnings
$$$

Job Outlook
Above-average increase

Painters & Paperhangers

On the Job

Painters and paperhangers make walls look clean and attractive by applying paint or wallpaper. They paint outside walls with special paints that protect the walls from weather damage. Painters mix paints to match colors, and then brush and roll the paints onto surfaces. Sometimes they rag-roll, splatter, or sponge on a second coat of paint in a different color. Paperhangers apply sizing and wallpapers and add decorative borders. Many are self-employed and work outdoors or seasonally.

SOMETHING EXTRA

It used to be that painters brushed and rolled a single color onto walls. Today, painters use a wide range of colors and techniques to jazz up walls. They might stencil, sponge, rag-roll, splatter, marbleize, or stipple paint onto a flat surface. They also use appliqué or wallpaper borders. A painter can act as a kind of interior decorator—limited only by his or her imagination.

Subjects to Study

Shop courses, art, math, physical education

Discover More

Try your painting skills by refinishing an old piece of furniture. First, sand off the old finish. Then clean the surface completely. Apply two or three even coats of a new color and then coat the surface with a clear finish.

Related Jobs

Carpenters; carpet, floor, and tile installers and finishers; drywall and ceiling tile installers, tapers, plasterers, and stucco masons; painting and coating workers, except construction and maintenance

Education & Training
Moderate-term OJT

Earnings
$$$

Job Outlook
Average increase

Plumbers, Pipelayers, Pipefitters & Steamfitters

On the Job

Plumbers install and repair water, waste disposal, drainage, and gas pipe systems in homes and other buildings. They install showers, sinks, toilets, and appliances. Pipelayers, pipefitters, and steamfitters install and repair the pipe systems used in manufacturing, electricity, and heating and cooling. These workers may work nights and weekends or be on call 24 hours a day. They must be strong enough to lift heavy pipes. Many are self-employed.

SOMETHING EXTRA

We may think of indoor plumbing as a modern convenience, or maybe we just take it for granted. But did you know that cultures as far back as 2600 B.C. had flush toilets attached to an elaborate sewage system? The Indus Valley civilization had one in nearly every house, paving the way for Egyptian plumbing advances and the Roman aqueducts.

Subjects to Study

Shop courses, drafting, blueprint reading, physics, physical education, math

Discover More

Tour your home or school and look at the pipe work in the bathrooms and kitchen. Are the pipes lead, stainless steel, plastic, or copper? Are the joints taped or welded? What other kinds of piping are in the building?

Related Jobs

Boilermakers; construction and building inspectors; construction managers; electricians; elevator installers and repairers; heating, air-conditioning, and refrigeration mechanics and installers; industrial machinery mechanics and millwrights; sheet metal workers; stationary engineers and boiler operators

Education & Training
Short-term OJT to Long-term OJT

Earnings
$$$

Job Outlook
Above-average increase

Roofers

On the Job

Roofers install roofs made of tar, asphalt, gravel, rubber, metal, and other materials. They may install or repair the shingles and tiles on home roofs and other buildings. Some roofers waterproof concrete walls and floors. These workers do physically demanding work outdoors, including lifting, climbing, and stooping. They risk injury from slips, falls, and burns.

SOMETHING EXTRA

In the 1970s, James Taylor re-recorded a song called "Up on the Roof." In it, Taylor sang about escaping from the worries of the world and sitting on the rooftop, just relaxing. In reality, rooftops can be steep, slippery, and scary places. They're not a good place for daydreaming, and roofing is not a good job for those who are careless or afraid of heights.

Subjects to Study

Shop courses, mechanical drawing, physical education, math

Discover More

Make a survey of roofing materials in your neighborhood. How many houses and buildings have asphalt-shingled roofs? Do any buildings in your area have metal roofs or wooden shingles? How many are missing shingles?

Related Jobs

Carpenters; carpet, floor, and tile installers and finishers; cement masons, concrete finishers, segmental pavers, and terrazzo workers; drywall and ceiling tile installers, tapers, plasterers, and stucco masons; sheet metal workers

Education & Training
Moderate-term OJT

Earnings
$$$

Job Outlook
Little change

Sheet Metal Workers

On the Job

Sheet metal workers use large sheets of metal to make duct-work for air-conditioning and heating systems. They make roofs, rain gutters, skylights, outdoor signs, and other products. They install and maintain these products as well. They usually work in shops or at the job site. They must be strong enough to lift heavy, bulky items. They wear safety glasses to protect their eyes. They cannot wear jewelry or loose-fitting clothing around their machinery.

SOMETHING EXTRA

You may know that many insulation workers in the 1970s were exposed to asbestos—an insulation that causes cancer in humans. But did you know that sheet metal workers had high exposures, too? In a survey taken in the late 1980s, more than 31 percent of sheet metal workers in construction, shipyard, and refinery work showed signs of asbestos-related diseases.

Subjects to Study

Algebra, geometry, mechanical drawing, shop courses, physical education

Discover More

To learn more about this job, write to the International Training Institute for the Sheet Metal and Air Conditioning Industry, 601 N. Fairfax St., Suite 240, Alexandria, VA 22314. Or you can visit their Web site at www.sheetmetal-iti.org.

Related Jobs

Assemblers and fabricators; glaziers; heating, air-conditioning, and refrigeration mechanics and installers; machine setters, operators, and tenders—metal and plastics; machinists; tool and die makers

Education & Training
Long-term OJT

Earnings
$$$

Job Outlook
Little change

Structural & Reinforcing Iron & Metal Workers

On the Job

These workers build the steel frames that strengthen bridges, high-rise buildings, highways, and other structures. They install metal stairways, window frames, decorative ironwork, and other metal products. Some erect metal storage tanks and other pre-made buildings. Structural and reinforcing metalworkers work outdoors in extremely high places, on scaffolding and beams. They must be strong enough to lift heavy metal.

SOMETHING EXTRA

It took 8,000 tons of steel, 93,167 high-strength bolts, and a 250-ton crane to build a 5,000-foot drawbridge. All that and just 15 people. That's right. A crew of 14 ironworkers and one crane operator built the bridge that connects the cities of Portland and South Portland, Maine. In only two months they laid almost 1,000 feet of girders—which just goes to show, experienced ironworkers can accomplish almost anything!

Subjects to Study

Shop courses, mechanical drawing, blueprint reading, physical education

Discover More

You can learn more about the physics of bridge building by making your own bridge. Stack four books in two piles that are the same height, four inches apart. Now use an index card as a bridge between the stacks. How many pennies can you put on the card before the "bridge" collapses? Now move the books closer and arch your bridge. Will it hold more pennies?

Education & Training
Long-term OJT

Earnings
$$$

Related Jobs

Assemblers and fabricators; boilermakers; carpenters; construction equipment operators; engineers; welding, soldering, and brazing workers

Job Outlook
Average increase

Installation, Maintenance & Repair Occupations

Computer, Automated Teller & Office Machine Repairers

On the Job

Computer repairers install and fix computers and related equipment. Office machine repairers work on copiers, cash registers, and fax machines. Some repairers work on both computers and office equipment. Automated teller repairers install and fix ATMs at banks and credit unions. These repairers work in many industries, and some are on call 24 hours a day to make emergency repairs.

SOMETHING EXTRA

Thomas Jefferson is famous for writing the Declaration of Independence, but did you know he was also an inventor? In fact, Jefferson invented the first copy machine. Here's how it worked. As the writer wrote a document with a pen connected to a machine, a second pen connected to the machine made another copy of the document. This early copy machine is on display at Jefferson's home in Charlottesville, Virginia.

Subjects to Study

Math, computer science, physics, shop, electronics

Discover More

Do you know how to hook up a computer? Ask the teacher in your school's computer lab to show you how to connect a computer's cables to the printer or scanner. Ask whether the school uses a power-surge protector to prevent electrical overload.

Related Jobs

Broadcast and sound engineering technicians and radio operators; electrical and electronics installers and repairers; electricians; electronic home entertainment equipment installers and repairers; home appliance repairers; maintenance and repair workers, general; radio and telecommunications equipment installers and repairers

Education & Training
Voc/tech training

Earnings
$$$

Job Outlook
Declining

Electrical & Electronics Installers & Repairers

On the Job

These workers install and repair equipment for power companies, governments, factories, hospitals, and other organizations. They work with electronic equipment, industrial controls, radar, missile controls, and communication systems. They may travel to factories or other locations to repair equipment. Others work in repair shops.

SOMETHING EXTRA

Since the first bands of nomads started arguing over territory, armies have been coming up with new ways to throw weapons at their enemies. During the Middle Ages, warriors used catapults to launch stones, dead horses, and even manure into enemy camps. Gunpowder and the first guns brought that kind of warfare to an end. Today's warriors use computers to guide missiles to their targets—which is a lot different than loading manure onto a catapult.

Subjects to Study

Math, physics, science, shop, electronics

Discover More

You can work on electronics projects in a science club or 4-H club. Ask your teacher whether one of these clubs meets at your school.

Related Jobs

Aircraft and avionics equipment mechanics and service technicians; broadcast and sound engineering technicians and radio operators; computer, automated teller, and office machine repairers; electricians; electronic home entertainment equipment installers and repairers; elevator installers and repairers; maintenance and repair workers, general; radio and telecommunications equipment installers and repairers

Education & Training
Voc/tech training

Earnings
$$$$

Job Outlook
Little change

Electronic Home Entertainment Equipment Installers & Repairers

On the Job

These workers install and repair audio and video equipment, such as televisions, stereo components, digital video disc players, and video cameras. They install and fix satellite television dishes and home theater systems. They sometimes use complex equipment to help them detect problems. Most work in repair shops or in service departments at larger stores. They may make home visits to fix equipment. Some are self-employed.

SOMETHING EXTRA

It can take decades for an invention to catch on with the public. For example, did you know that push-button phones were first invented in 1896? And color television was first demonstrated in 1929? But until the 1960s, neither item was in common use in America. What technology is out there today, waiting for us to notice? We might not know for years!

Subjects to Study

Math, science, shop, electronics, physics

Discover More

Visit a home electronics repair department or shop in your area. Ask the technicians whether you can watch as they make repairs and run tests.

Related Jobs

Computer, automated teller, and office machine repairers; electrical and electronics installers and repairers; electricians; home appliance repairers; maintenance and repair workers, general; radio and telecommunications equipment installers and repairers

Education & Training
Voc/tech training

Earnings
$$$

Job Outlook
Average increase

Radio & Telecommunications Equipment Installers & Repairers

On the Job

These workers install, repair, and maintain complex telephone, radio, and Internet equipment. Most work either in a phone company's central office or in the field at customers' homes or offices. Others work on equipment for cable TV companies, railroads, or airlines. Some work nights and weekends, and they may be on call to handle emergencies.

SOMETHING EXTRA

Communications equipment has changed a lot in the last 100 years. Before 1876, if you wanted to get in touch with people across town, you had to write a letter or go to their house. Today, you can connect with people in Mongolia or Zimbabwe instantly by phone or through the Internet. We have become a global village.

Subjects to Study

Math, science courses, shop, electronics, physics

Discover More

Take apart an old telephone and look at its insides. Can you follow the wires to their sources? Can you figure out what the different parts do? Now, can you put it back together?

Related Jobs

Broadcast and sound engineering technicians and radio operators; computer, automated teller, and office machine repairers; electrical and electronics installers and repairers; engineering technicians; line installers and repairers

Education & Training
Voc/tech training

Earnings
$$$$

Job Outlook
Declining

Aircraft & Avionics Equipment Mechanics & Service Technicians

On the Job

Aircraft and avionics mechanics and service technicians inspect airplanes for problems. They make repairs and test equipment to make sure it is working properly. Some work on several different types of planes, whereas others specialize in just one type. Some mechanics even specialize in one part of an aircraft, such as the engine or electrical system of a Boeing 787. Sometimes they work inside, but often they work outdoors.

SOMETHING EXTRA

How safe is air travel? Statistics show that a good percentage of Americans are afraid to fly, but those same people often don't think twice about driving on the interstate. Yet according to the U.S. National Safety Council, you are 20 times more likely to be killed in an auto accident than in an airplane accident. So maybe you should start taking a chartered jet to school each day.

Subjects to Study

Math, physics, chemistry, electronics, computer science, mechanical drawing

Discover More

To find out more about aircraft mechanics, write to the Flight Safety Foundation, 601 Madison Street, Suite 300, Alexandria, VA 22314. Or visit its Web site at www.flightsafety.org.

Related Jobs

Automotive service technicians and mechanics; electrical and electronics installers and repairers; electricians; elevator installers and repairers

Education & Training
Voc/tech training

Earnings
$$$$

Job Outlook
Average increase

Automotive Body & Related Repairers

On the Job

Automotive body repairers fix cars and trucks damaged in accidents. They straighten bent bodies, hammer out dents, and replace parts that can't be fixed. Their supervisors usually decide which parts to fix, which ones to replace, and how long the job should take. In large shops, some repairers specialize in one type of repair, such as installing glass or repairing doors.

SOMETHING EXTRA

Did you know that some cars have parts made from plastic? If these parts are damaged, a body repairer can use heat from a hot-air welding gun or simply put the damaged part in very hot water to make the plastic soft. Then the repairer can mold the softened part into its original shape and put it back on the car.

Subjects to Study

Shop, automotive body repair, science courses, math

Discover More

A model car has many of the same body parts as a real car. Buy a model car kit and build and paint the model. Can you customize the car so that it reflects your personality?

Related Jobs

Automotive service technicians and mechanics; diesel service technicians and mechanics; glaziers; heavy vehicle and mobile equipment service technicians and mechanics; painting and coating workers, except construction and maintenance

Education & Training
Long-term OJT

Earnings
$$$

Job Outlook
Little change

Automotive Service Technicians & Mechanics

On the Job

Automotive mechanics and service technicians repair and service cars, trucks, and other vehicles that have gas engines. Mechanics must be quick and accurate when they are diagnosing mechanical problems. During routine service work, mechanics inspect, adjust, and replace vehicle parts. They usually follow a checklist to make sure they examine parts that might cause a future breakdown. Some mechanics are self-employed. This job is becoming more technically demanding as automobiles become more complex.

SOMETHING EXTRA

You've probably heard of the Indy 500. It's one of the biggest events of the year for racing pros. But you might not know just how expensive it is to race a car at Indy. For example, pit-crew mechanics change all four tires on a racecar seven times during each race. And each set of tires costs $1,200. That's $8,400 in tires alone. What do you suppose it costs to replace an engine?

Subjects to Study

Math, shop, automotive mechanics, electronics, computer skills

Discover More

Do you know someone who works on cars? Ask that person whether you can help or just watch while he or she works on a car. You can learn a lot by watching and listening as a mechanic works. You might be able to help by handing him or her tools.

Education & Training
Voc/tech training

Earnings
$$$

Related Jobs

Automotive body and related repairers, diesel service technicians and mechanics, heavy vehicle and mobile equipment service technicians and mechanics, small engine mechanics

Job Outlook
Little change

Diesel Service Technicians & Mechanics

On the Job

Diesel mechanics and service technicians repair and maintain diesel engines in heavy trucks, buses, tractors, bulldozers, and cranes. They spend a lot of time doing preventive maintenance to make sure that the equipment operates safely, to prevent wear and tear, and to reduce expensive breakdowns. Most work in repair shops, but some work outdoors to repair equipment at construction sites.

SOMETHING EXTRA

Diesel engines are heavier and last longer than gas engines. They're also more efficient because a diesel engine compresses its fuel—so it uses less to do more. This means that more fuel is available to power the engine. Large trucks, buses, trains, and even some cars have diesel engines. Although diesel fuel is more efficient, it might be harder to find at your local gas station.

Subjects to Study

Math, shop, automotive repair, electronics, computer skills

Discover More

Do you know the differences between gas engines and diesel engines? You can find out by reading about engines and how they work. Check out some science books from the library and learn about both kinds of engines. Or research it at www.howstuffworks.com/diesel1.htm.

Related Jobs

Aircraft and avionics equipment mechanics and service technicians, automotive body and related repairers, automotive service technicians and mechanics, heavy vehicle and mobile equipment service technicians and mechanics, small engine mechanics

Education & Training
Voc/tech training

Earnings
$$$

Job Outlook
Little change

Heavy Vehicle & Mobile Equipment Service Technicians & Mechanics

On the Job

These mechanics and technicians repair the machinery used in construction, logging, and mining. They fix and maintain motor graders, trenchers, backhoes, bulldozers, and cranes. They service and repair diesel engines and other machine parts. They may repair the hydraulic lifts used to raise and lower scoops and shovels. These workers are outdoors in all kinds of weather.

SOMETHING EXTRA

When a big piece of machinery breaks down at a logging site or a mine, the workers can't pack it up and bring it into the repair shop. That's where a field service mechanic comes in. These workers drive specially equipped trucks to the work site to make the repair. They might be on the job for a week or two before they're off to the next site. Many mechanics enjoy the independence of working outside the repair shop.

Subjects to Study

Math, automobile mechanics, physics, chemistry, shop

Discover More

Visit a construction site and watch how the equipment moves and works. Talk to a construction worker about what happens when a machine breaks down.

Related Jobs

Aircraft and avionics equipment mechanics and service technicians, automotive service technicians and mechanics, diesel service technicians and mechanics, industrial machinery mechanics and millwrights, small engine mechanics

Education & Training
Long-term OJT

Earnings
$$$

Job Outlook
Average increase

Small Engine Mechanics

On the Job

Small engine mechanics do routine engine checkups and repair everything from chainsaws to yachts. The mechanic first talks with the owner to understand the problem. Then he or she runs tests to find the source of the problem. In some areas, mechanics may work much more during the summer than they do in the winter because use of motorcycles, boats, and lawnmowers is more frequent. Many of these workers are self-employed.

SOMETHING EXTRA

If you take a job in a restaurant, you wouldn't expect to bring your own pots and pans, would you? But mechanics often must provide their own hand tools for their work. Most beginning mechanics start out with the basics, such as wrenches, pliers, screwdrivers, and power drills. As they gain experience, they collect more tools. Experienced mechanics might have thousands of dollars invested in tools.

Subjects to Study

Math, small-engine repair, shop, science, electronics

Discover More

Ask your parents or neighbor whether you can help them prepare the lawnmower for spring use or winter storage. As you work, ask about the various parts of the motor.

Related Jobs

Automotive service technicians and mechanics, diesel service technicians and mechanics, heavy vehicle and mobile equipment service technicians and mechanics, home appliance repairers

Education & Training
Moderate-term OJT
to Long-term OJT

Earnings
$$

Job Outlook
Average increase

Heating, Air-Conditioning & Refrigeration Mechanics & Installers

On the Job

These mechanics help keep people comfortable by installing and repairing heating systems and air conditioners. They protect food and medicine that must be kept refrigerated. These workers maintain, diagnose, and correct problems within entire heating or cooling systems. They may work for large companies or be self-employed. They must conform to strict guidelines to help protect the environment.

SOMETHING EXTRA

People working in this job can have a strong impact on the environment. CFCs are coolants used in older air-conditioning and refrigeration systems. Particles of CFCs are dangerous if they escape into the atmosphere. Escaped CFCs eat away at the ozone layer that protects plants, animals, and people from too much radiation. Nothing on Earth will survive if the ozone layer is completely destroyed. Responsible technicians are careful to protect the environment from CFCs.

Subjects to Study

Shop, math, electronics, mechanical drawing, physics, chemistry, blueprint reading, physical education

Discover More

Visit a supermarket and ask to talk with someone who works in the frozen-food or dairy section. Ask how repairs are made to the cooling systems.

Related Jobs

Boilermakers; electricians; home appliance repairers; plumbers, pipelayers, pipefitters, and steamfitters; sheet metal workers

Education & Training
Voc/tech training

Earnings
$$$

Job Outlook
Rapid increase

Home Appliance Repairers

On the Job

These workers repair ovens, washers, dryers, refrigerators, and other home appliances. They may repair power tools such as saws and drills. First, they find the problem. Then they replace or repair faulty parts. At the same time, they tighten, clean, and adjust other parts if needed. They must keep good records, prepare bills, and collect payments.

SOMETHING EXTRA

Though iceboxes had been used for centuries to keep things cold, the first practical refrigerator was developed by an Australian journalist named James Harrison. Because it wasn't cold enough in Australia to harvest and store ice, Harrison was commissioned by a brewery in 1856 to design a refrigeration system. Thus, time-travelers headed back to 19th century Australia would open the door of the first fridge to find it full of beer.

Subjects to Study

Shop courses, electronics, math, science

Discover More

Call a repair shop in your area and ask whether you can help in the shop for a day or two. Watch how the repairer works. Help out by bringing tools, waiting on customers, or cleaning the shop.

Related Jobs

Coin, vending, and amusement machine servicers and repairers; electrical and electronics installers and repairers; electronic home entertainment equipment installers and repairers; heating, air-conditioning, and refrigeration mechanics and installers; small engine mechanics

Education & Training
Long-term OJT

Earnings
$$$

Job Outlook
Little change

Industrial Machinery Mechanics & Millwrights

On the Job

Industrial machinery workers install and maintain the machines in factories or plants to keep the work on schedule. Their work includes keeping machines and parts oiled, tuned, and cleaned. When repairs are needed, the repairer must work quickly so that production is not delayed. Sometimes this means making emergency repairs at night or on weekends. Millwrights install, repair, replace, and take apart the machinery and heavy equipment used in many industries.

SOMETHING EXTRA

Industrial machinery mechanics must be able to spot and fix little problems before they cause major breakdowns. If a machine has a vibration that shouldn't be there, mechanics must find the source of the problem, such as a worn belt or loose bearing. The more repairs they make at early stages, the more money they save their employers down the road.

Subjects to Study

Mechanical drawing, math, blueprint reading, science, physics, shop, electronics, physical education, computer skills

Discover More

Contact the office of a factory in your area and ask for a tour. Watch the machinery used in production. Ask your guide what would happen to the production schedule if an important piece of machinery broke down.

Related Jobs

Electrical and electronics installers and repairers; electricians; machinists; maintenance and repair workers, general; plumbers, pipelayers, pipefitters, and steamfitters; welding, soldering, and brazing workers

Education & Training
Moderate-term OJT to Long-term OJT

Earnings
$$$

Job Outlook
Little change

Line Installers & Repairers

On the Job

Line installers and repairers lay the wires and cables that bring electricity, phone service, Internet service, and cable TV signals into homes. They clear lines of tree limbs, check them for damage, and make emergency repairs when needed. This job can be dangerous because installers and splicers work underground, high above ground, and with various chemicals and electricity. They work outside in all kinds of weather.

> ## SOMETHING EXTRA
>
> How much information can pass through a cable as wide as a human hair? A lot! Fiber-optic cables are made of tiny strands of glass. These tiny strands carry electricity, phone service, and cable TV signals to homes and businesses. So powerful are these strands that one pair of optical fibers can carry more than 100,000 phone conversations at one time!

Subjects to Study

Math, physical education, shop courses, science courses, electronics

Discover More

Contact the human resources department of your local electric company, telephone company, or cable TV company. Ask about the kinds of jobs they have and what kind of training they require.

Related Jobs

Electrical and electronics installers and repairers; electricians; power plant operators, distributors, and dispatchers; radio and telecommunications equipment installers and repairers

Education & Training
Long-term OJT

Earnings
$$$$

Job Outlook
Little change

Maintenance & Repair Workers, General

On the Job

General maintenance and repair workers have skills in many crafts. They repair and maintain machines, mechanical equipment, and buildings. They work on plumbing, electrical, and air-conditioning and heating systems. They build partitions; make drywall repairs; fix roofs; and paint and repair windows, doors, floors, woodwork, and other parts of buildings. They maintain and repair specialized equipment and machinery found in cafeterias, laundries, hospitals, stores, offices, and factories.

SOMETHING EXTRA

Just about everyone needs to know something about computers, including general maintenance workers. New buildings sometimes have computer-controlled systems, requiring workers to acquire basic computer skills. For example, new air-conditioning systems often can be controlled from a central computer terminal. General maintenance workers have yet another skill to add to their vast repertoire.

Subjects to Study

Mechanical drawing, electricity, woodworking, blueprint reading, science, math, computer skills

Discover More

Spend a day on the job with your school custodian. You'll find that custodians do much more than sweep the halls. They are responsible for making sure all the machinery in your school works properly.

Related Jobs

Boilermakers; carpenters; electrical and electronics installers and repairers; electricians; heating, air-conditioning, and refrigeration mechanics and installers; plumbers, pipelayers, pipefitters, and steamfitters

Education & Training
Moderate-term OJT

Earnings
$$$

Job Outlook
Average increase

Medical Equipment Repairers

On the Job

Medical equipment repairers adjust and fix a wide variety of equipment in hospitals and other medical environments. They work on patient monitors, defibrillators, X-rays, CAT scanners, ultrasound equipment, voice-controlled operating tables, and electric wheelchairs. They repair sophisticated dental, optometric, and ophthalmic equipment. Medical equipment repairers use a wide variety of tools.

SOMETHING EXTRA

What's it like to work as a medical equipment repairer? They work in a patient environment, which could expose them to diseases and other health risks. Because medical equipment is often used in life-saving treatments, fixing equipment can be urgent. Although this may be gratifying, it can also be very stressful and require overtime. Those who work as contractors often have to travel—sometimes long distances—to perform repairs.

Subjects to Study

Computer skills, shop, science, math, electronics

Discover More

Do you have a grandparent or other relative with a pacemaker? Do you know someone who checks his sugar readings every day with a glucose meter? Research these devices online to learn how they work.

Related Jobs

Computer, automated teller, and office machine repairers; medical, dental, and ophthalmic laboratory technicians

Education & Training
Associate degree

Earnings
$$$

Job Outlook
Rapid increase

Production Occupations

Assemblers & Fabricators

On the Job

Assemblers and fabricators are experienced and trained workers who put together complicated products such as computers, appliances, and electronic equipment. Their work is detailed and must be done accurately. They follow directions from engineers. They use tools and precise measuring instruments. Some work in clean, well-lit rooms, while others work around grease, oil, and noise. They may have to lift and fit heavy objects.

Subjects to Study

Math, science, computer education, shop courses, electronics

Discover More

Get a kit from an electronics store and assemble a radio or another piece of electronic equipment. Or build a model car, plane, or rocket to develop your assembly skills.

Related Jobs

Industrial machinery mechanics and millwrights; inspectors, testers, sorters, samplers, and weighers; machine setters, operators, and tenders—metal and plastic; welding, soldering, and brazing workers

Education & Training
Short-term OJT to Moderate-term OJT

Earnings
$$

Job Outlook
Declining

Food Processing Occupations

On the Job

Food processing workers work in grocery stores and production plants. They may work in a small market, in a large refrigerated room, or on an assembly line. Their work areas must be clean, but they are often cold and damp.

SOMETHING EXTRA

In the 1800s, a Swiss naturalist connected two facts. First, the brain contains phosphorus. Second, phosphorus is found in fish. Therefore, he decided that eating fish helps develop the brain. Actually, phosphorus is found in most foods, so eating fish before a test isn't a guarantee of getting an A. But it can't hurt!

Bakers produce cakes, breads, and other baked goods. Deli workers make salads and side dishes. Butchers and meat, poultry, and fish cutters cut food into small pieces to be sold to customers.

Subjects to Study

Health, science courses, nutrition, family and consumer sciences, food preparation

Discover More

Learn about the different cuts of meat, fish, and poultry. Visit the meat department of a grocery store to see the different cuts. Talk to the butcher and ask about the job.

Related Jobs

Chefs, head cooks, and food preparation and serving supervisors; cooks and food preparation workers

Education & Training
Short-term OJT to Long-term OJT

Earnings
$$

Job Outlook
Little change

Computer Control Programmers & Operators

On the Job

These workers use special computer-controlled machines to cut and shape products such as car parts, machine parts, and compressors. They follow blueprints from engineers. While they work, they must constantly monitor readouts from the computer to make sure parts are being made properly. Because of the machinery, this job can be dangerous.

SOMETHING EXTRA

Many metal and plastics workers learn their trades through an apprenticeship program. They start by working with a professional, making little money but gaining invaluable experience. When the apprenticeship is finished, the new workers become tradesmen or journeymen, a title that lets people know they have a certain set of skills. Apprenticeships are a time-honored way to learn a profession. No one knows for certain when they began, but they are mentioned in many ancient texts, including the Bible.

Subjects to Study

Math, shop, blueprint reading, drafting, physics, mechanical drawing, computer skills, electronics

Discover More

Visit a machining shop in your community and watch the programmers and operators at work. You may be able to help by watching monitors and carrying parts.

Related Jobs

Computer software engineers and computer programmers; industrial machinery mechanics and millwrights; machinists; machine setters, operators, and tenders—metal and plastic; tool and die makers; welding, soldering, and brazing workers

Education & Training
Moderate-term OJT to Work experience

Earnings
$$$

Job Outlook
Little change

Machine Setters, Operators & Tenders—Metal & Plastics

On the Job

These workers fall into two groups: those who set up machines for operation, and those who tend the machines while they work. They may work with drilling and boring machines, milling and planing machines, or lathe and turning machines. They work according to blueprints and other instructions to turn out metal and plastic parts for everything from toasters to trucks.

SOMETHING EXTRA

These jobs have been greatly affected by computers and advances in technology. In the past, workers had to set each machine by hand, measuring each part to ensure that it met the blueprints. Today, computers do much of the work, from setting the size on machines to measuring the finished parts. Of course, those computers don't operate on their own. Trained professionals ensure that production goes smoothly.

Subjects to Study

Math, shop, blueprint reading, drafting, physics, computer skills, electronics

Discover More

Take apart an old appliance at home, such as a toaster or alarm clock. Be sure to unplug it first. Separate the appliance into as many individual pieces as possible. Now look at the variety of shapes and sizes. Each part was made by machine setters and tenders.

Related Jobs

Assemblers and fabricators; computer control programmers and operators; machinists; painting and coating workers, except construction and maintenance; tool and die makers; welding, soldering, and brazing workers

Education & Training
Moderate-term OJT
to Long-term OJT

Earnings
$$

Job Outlook
Declining

Machinists

On the Job

Machinists make metal parts using lathes, drill presses, and milling machines. They make specialized parts or one-of-a-kind items for companies that produce everything from cars to computers. Most work in machine shops and wear safety glasses and ear-plugs. Because of the machinery they use and the coolants and lubricants for the machine, this can be a dangerous job.

Subjects to Study

Math, shop, blueprint reading, drafting, physics, mechanical drawing, computer skills, electronics

Discover More

High school shops and vocational schools are some places you can find metalworking machines. Ask the instructor to show you how the machines work.

Related Jobs

Computer control programmers and operators; industrial machinery mechanics and millwrights; machine setters, operators, and tenders—metal and plastics; tool and die makers

Education & Training
Long-term OJT

Earnings
$$$

Job Outlook
Declining

Tool & Die Makers

On the Job

Tool and die makers are highly skilled workers. Tool-makers create tools that cut, shape, and form metal and other materials. Die makers make dies, which are the forms used to shape metal in stamping and forging machines. Tool and die makers must know about machining operations, mathematics, and blueprint reading. They must follow safety rules and wear protective clothing. They spend a good part of the day standing and must be able to lift heavy items.

Subjects to Study

Math, shop, blueprint reading, drafting, mechanical drawing

Discover More

Using pen and paper, design a new tool to do something useful. Or think up a new use for an old tool. Can you convert an egg slicer to cut bagel chips? Can you think of a better tool for opening jars or cans?

Related Jobs

Computer control programmers and operators; industrial machinery mechanics and millwrights; machine setters, operators, and tenders—metal and plastics; machinists; welding, soldering, and brazing workers

Education & Training
Long-term OJT

Earnings
$$$$

Job Outlook
Declining

Welding, Soldering & Brazing Workers

On the Job

These workers use the heat from a torch to permanently join metal parts. Because of its strength, welding is used to build ships, cars, aircraft, and space shuttles. Welders may use a hand torch or a welding machine. They use torches to cut and dismantle metal objects. Welders must wear protective gear such as safety shoes and hoods with protective lenses to prevent burns and injuries. Some work outdoors on ladders or scaffolding.

SOMETHING EXTRA

Say the word *welder*, and many people think of a guy in a hard hat and goggles. But many of today's welders are women, and they can trace their history to World War II. During the war, the shipyards of San Francisco were so short of workers that they began hiring and training housewives and mothers to do jobs traditionally held by men. These "lady welders" in overalls had a popular song written and named for them: "Rosie the Riveter."

Subjects to Study

Shop, blueprint reading, mechanical drawing, physics, chemistry

Discover More

To learn more about this occupation, write to the American Welding Society, 550 N.W. LeJeune Rd., Miami, FL 33126. Or check out its Web site at www.aws.org.

Related Jobs

Assemblers and fabricators; boilermakers; computer control programmers and operators; jewelers and precious stone and metal workers; machine setters, operators, and tenders—metal and plastic; machinists; plumbers, pipelayers, pipefitters, and steamfitters; sheet metal workers; tool and die makers

Education & Training
Voc/tech training

Earnings
$$$

Job Outlook
Declining

Bookbinders & Bindery Workers

On the Job

Bookbinders and bindery workers use machines to bind the pages of books and magazines in a cover. These machines fold, cut, gather, glue, stitch, sew, trim, and wrap pages to form a book. Bindery work is physically hard. Workers stand, kneel, lift, and carry heavy items. Many work on assembly lines. Some work in hand binderies, and a few are self-employed.

SOMETHING EXTRA

Did you know that some rare old books are worth hundreds of thousands of dollars? So what does a library or museum do when one of these treasures starts to fall apart? They call a bookbinder. These workers use special tools and chemicals to restore pages. Then they rebind the book by hand, using needle and thread. To help prevent books from deteriorating, many rare book libraries require patrons to sit in environmentally controlled rooms and wear gloves.

Subjects to Study

Math, English, art, shop courses

Discover More

Bind your own book. First make an "end paper" by folding a sheet of heavy paper over your pages. Sew the pages into the end paper, using a heavy thread and needle. Paste each end paper to a heavy cardboard square. Now paste the squares onto a sheet of wallpaper. Cut the wallpaper to leave one inch of trim. Fold the trim over the cardboard squares and paste them down to make your book.

Education & Training
Short-term OJT to Moderate-term OJT

Earnings
$$

Related Jobs

Machine setters, operators, and tenders—metal and plastic; prepress technicians and workers; printing machine operators

Job Outlook
Declining

Prepress Technicians & Workers

On the Job

Prepress technicians and workers prepare materials for printing presses. They do typesetting, design page layouts, take photographs, and make printing plates. With personal computers, customers can now show workers how they want their printed material to look. Prepress workers have different titles depending on their jobs. Most work at video monitors, but some work with harmful chemicals.

SOMETHING EXTRA

Desktop publishing has changed the printing industry and the jobs of prepress workers. Today, they use computer programs to design and prepare materials for printing. These programs allow workers to separate color photos into the four basic colors that all printers use. The computer tells the printer precisely how much of each ink color to apply so that the blend matches the original photos exactly.

Subjects to Study

English, electronics, computer skills, art, photography

Discover More

Learn how to use word processing and graphics programs on a computer. Design your own greeting card, newsletter, or brochure.

Related Jobs

Artists and related workers, bookbinders and bindery workers, desktop publishers, graphic designers, printing machine operators

Education & Training
Long-term OJT to Voc/tech training

Earnings
$$$

Job Outlook
Declining

Printing Machine Operators

On the Job

Printing machine operators prepare, run, and maintain the printing presses in a pressroom. They check the paper and ink, make sure paper feeders are stocked, and monitor the presses as they run. Computerized presses allow operators to make adjustments at a control panel by simply pressing buttons. These workers are on their feet most of the time. The work can be loud and physically demanding.

SOMETHING EXTRA

Before the Middle Ages, few people could read. That's because manuscripts had to be copied by hand. A group of workers called scribes were employed by monasteries to copy books. It was a time-consuming and expensive process. When a man named Gutenberg made the first printing press in 1456, he put a lot of scribes out of work. But he also made books available to the common man for the first time. Gutenberg's printing press is considered to be one of the most important inventions in human history.

Subjects to Study

Math, English, computer science, chemistry, electronics, physics

Discover More

Try printing your own greeting cards with a woodblock printing kit. These kits are available at craft and hobby stores.

Related Jobs

Bookbinders and bindery workers; machine setters, operators, and tenders—metal and plastics; prepress technicians and workers

Education & Training
Moderate-term OJT

Earnings
$$$

Job Outlook
Declining

Textile, Apparel & Furnishings Occupations

On the Job

Textile workers care for and operate the machines that make textile goods. These goods are then used in all kinds of products, from clothing to materials used in tires. Apparel workers make cloth, leather, and fur into clothing and other products. They may repair torn or damaged items, or resew them to fit a customer better. Upholsterers are skilled craft workers who make new furniture or repair old furniture.

SOMETHING EXTRA

Have you heard the term child labor? In the past, many children worked in the apparel industry in this country. Children working in spinning houses began their days at 5 a.m. and worked 13 hours a day. Often, they received only two meals a day. Today, child labor laws forbid such conditions in the U.S. But in other parts of the world, children work long days for low wages.

Subjects to Study

Family and consumer sciences, sewing, shop, woodworking, art, math, computer skills

Discover More

Get a pattern for a simple sewing project. Follow the pattern directions to make something you can wear.

Related Jobs

Assemblers and fabricators; food processing occupations; jewelers and precious stone and metal workers; woodworkers

Education & Training
Short-term OJT to Long-term OJT

Earnings
$

Job Outlook
Declining

Woodworkers

On the Job

Woodworkers make things from wood and work in many stages of the production process. They use machines that cut, shape, assemble, and finish wood to make doors, cabinets, paneling, and furniture. Precision woodworkers use hand tools to make rare or customized items. Most woodworkers handle heavy materials, stand for long periods, and risk exposure to dust and air pollutants. Some operate dangerous equipment.

SOMETHING EXTRA

If you think woodworkers make only furniture, think again! Woodworkers create a huge variety of items, from cabinets and rocking chairs to fishing decoys and jewelry. Some specialize in musical instruments such as guitars and banjoes. Others make knickknacks such as wooden flowers and jewelry boxes. Woodworkers even make machines from wood—imagine a wooden paper shredder. In fact, if you can dream it, a woodworker can probably make it.

Subjects to Study

Math, computer skills, shop, woodworking, blueprint reading

Discover More

Ask an adult to help you with a woodworking project, such as building a shelf or a wooden toy. You can get plans and materials for these projects at a hardware store.

Related Jobs

Carpenters, computer control programmers and operators, machinists, sheet metal workers, structural and reinforcing iron and metal workers

Education & Training
Moderate-term OJT to Long-term OJT

Earnings
$$

Job Outlook
Little change

Power Plant Operators, Distributors & Dispatchers

On the Job

Power plant operators control the machinery that generates electricity. They start or stop generators as power requirements change. Power distributors and dispatchers make sure that users receive enough electricity by planning for times when more electricity is needed and handling emergencies. These workers often work nights, weekends, and holidays.

SOMETHING EXTRA

Why would a power plant dispatcher need to know the weather forecast? Because dispatchers must plan ahead to meet people's needs for electricity. During a heat wave, when everyone is running an air conditioner, the plant must provide more electricity. During blizzards, it must provide enough power to run furnaces and heaters that are working overtime. Dispatchers must be prepared for emergencies such as downed power lines.

Subjects to Study

Math, physics, electronics, computer science, shop, English

Discover More

Talk to someone at the public relations department of your local electric company. Find out where your electricity is generated. Can your class take a field trip to tour the plant?

Related Jobs

Electrical and electronics installers and repairers, electricians, line installers and repairers, stationary engineers and boiler operators, water and liquid waste treatment plant and system operators

Education & Training
Long-term OJT

Earnings
$$$$

Job Outlook
Little change

Stationary Engineers & Boiler Operators

On the Job

Stationary engineers and boiler operators run and maintain equipment that provides air-conditioning, heat, and ventilation to large buildings. This equipment may supply electricity, steam, or other types of power. These workers may work weekends and holidays. They are exposed to heat, dust, dirt, and noise from the equipment. Hazards of the job include burns, electric shock, and injury from moving machinery parts.

Subjects to Study

Math, computer science, mechanical drawing, shop, chemistry

Discover More

Learn how to maintain machines in your home, such as the lawnmower and electric tools. Learn what tools to use, how to oil the machines, and how to keep them in good repair.

Education & Training
Long-term OJT

Related Jobs

Industrial machinery mechanics and millwrights; maintenance and repair workers, general; power plant operators, distributors, and dispatchers; water and liquid waste treatment plant and system operators

Earnings
$$$$

Job Outlook
Little change

Water & Liquid Waste Treatment Plant & System Operators

On the Job

Water treatment plant operators make sure that the water you drink is safe. Wastewater plant operators remove harmful pollution from wastewater. They read meters and gauges and adjust controls. They take water samples, perform analyses, and adjust chemicals in the water, such as chlorine. They work indoors and outdoors and may be exposed to dangerous gases. They may work day, evening, or night shifts; weekends; and holidays.

SOMETHING EXTRA

One of the hottest topics in water treatment today is desalination—the process of converting ocean and seawater into drinkable water. This process removes the salt and other minerals from the water so that people can use it for tap water. It is an expensive process but a necessary one in places such as the Middle East, where fresh water is scarce. Scientists are looking at the possibility of using the process in California, too.

Subjects to Study

Math, chemistry, biology, shop, health, environmental sciences

Discover More

Call the water company in your community and ask whether your class can participate in a water-testing program. Many companies will send a representative to your school to teach a class how to test the water in your home for pollutants such as lead and harmful bacteria.

Related Jobs

Power plant operators, distributors, and dispatchers; stationary engineers and boiler operators

Education & Training
Long-term OJT

Earnings
$$$$

Job Outlook
Average increase

Inspectors, Testers, Sorters, Samplers & Weighers

On the Job

These workers examine and sort products before releasing them to consumers. They may test by looking, listening, feeling, tasting, weighing, or smelling. Products must meet quality standards. Inspectors may reject a product, send it back to be fixed, or fix the problem themselves. Inspectors work in all kinds of industries. Some move from place to place. Others sit on an assembly line all day.

SOMETHING EXTRA

How does a toy company ensure that each toy it produces is well made and safe for children? It hires inspectors to test them. A toy inspector might poke, pull, and drop a toy to see whether it breaks. The inspector may measure it to see whether it could be a choking hazard for young children. Inspectors work in every industry that produces an item for sale. If a product is later found to have a defect, it has to be recalled and replaced at great cost to the company.

Subjects to Study

English, math, shop, blueprint reading, computer skills

Discover More

Learn how to contact a company if you are not satisfied with a product. Check the packaging of food for a consumer telephone number or Web site. Contact the company to learn what it would do if you were not happy with the product.

Related Jobs

Construction and building inspectors, occupational health and safety specialists, occupational health and safety technicians

Education & Training
Moderate-term OJT

Earnings
$$

Job Outlook
Rapid increase

Jewelers & Precious Stone & Metal Workers

On the Job

These workers use precious metals and stones such as gold and diamonds to make necklaces, rings, bracelets, and other jewelry. Some specialize in one area, such as buying, designing, cutting, repairing, selling, or appraising jewels. This work requires a high degree of skill and attention to detail. Jewelers use chemicals, sawing and drilling tools, and torches in their work. Some are self-employed.

SOMETHING EXTRA

One of the most famous jewels in the world is the Hope Diamond. This 451-carat blue diamond was found in the early 1600s and has crossed oceans and continents and passed from kings to commoners. But its fame is due to the bad luck it seems to bring its owners. More than 20 deaths have been blamed on the gem. Several of its owners have been killed by wild dogs, been beheaded, or committed suicide. You can see it at the Smithsonian Natural History Museum in Washington, D.C.

Subjects to Study

Math, art, mechanical drawing, chemistry, computer skills, blueprint reading

Discover More

Take a jewelry-making class at school or your local craft store. Try designing and selling your own jewelry pieces.

Related Jobs

Artists and related workers; commercial and industrial designers; fashion designers; retail salespersons; sales representatives, wholesale and manufacturing; welding, soldering, and brazing workers; woodworkers

Education & Training
Voc/tech training

Earnings
$$$

Job Outlook
Little change

Medical, Dental & Ophthalmic Laboratory Technicians

On the Job

Medical laboratory technicians construct artificial limbs, braces, and supports based on prescriptions from doctors. Dental laboratory technicians make the products dentists use to replace decayed teeth. Using dentists' directions and molds of patients' mouths, they make dentures (false teeth), crowns, and bridges. Ophthalmic laboratory technicians make the lenses for eyeglasses or for instruments like telescopes and binoculars.

SOMETHING EXTRA

What did people do before they had porcelain dentures? Did you know that when Elizabeth I was queen of England (1558–1603), she lost her front teeth to decay? To make her face appear fuller, Elizabeth put pieces of cloth under her lips. Other members of the royal court had ornamental teeth made from silver or gold. The first "dentures" were made from bone or ivory, or created from the teeth of dead or even living donors!

Subjects to Study

Science, art, shop, drafting, business, math

Discover More

Visit an optical store at your local mall. Most have ophthalmic labs on site. Ask whether you can watch the technician work on a pair of glasses. Try on some frames while you're there.

Related Jobs

Dentists; medical equipment repairers; opticians, dispensing; optometrists; orthotists and prosthetists; textile, apparel, and furnishings occupations

Education & Training
Moderate-term OJT to Long-term OJT

Earnings
$$

Job Outlook
Above-average increase

Painting & Coating Workers, Except Construction & Maintenance

On the Job

Painting and coating machine operators cover everything from cars to candy with paints, plastics, varnishes, chocolates, or special solutions. The most common methods of applying paints and coatings are spraying and dipping. These workers wear respirators over their noses and mouths to protect themselves from dangerous fumes. Most work in factories, but self-employed car painters have their own shops.

SOMETHING EXTRA

You probably can think of things that are painted—cars, toys, bikes, and wicker furniture. But what does a coating machine do? Well, paper-coating machines apply the glossy finish on paper products. Silvering applicators spray a mix of silver, copper, and tin onto glass to make mirrors. And enrobing machines coat bakery goods with melted chocolate, sugar, or cheese. So the same skills that might help you paint a car can also help you make a Milky Way.

Subjects to Study

Shop, art, chemistry

Discover More

You can watch spray painting in action at an auto body repair shop. Call a shop and ask if you can watch the painters. You will probably have to watch from a distance because of the fumes.

Related Jobs

Automotive body and related repairers; machine setters, operators, and tenders—metal and plastics; painters and paperhangers

Education & Training
Short-term OJT to Moderate-term OJT

Earnings
$$

Job Outlook
Little change

Semiconductor Processors

On the Job

Semiconductors, also known as microchips, are the tiny brains inside computers. Semiconductor processors are the workers who make these microchips. They work in sterile areas and wear special coveralls called "bunny suits" to keep dust away from the chips. Operators use special equipment to imprint information on tiny silicon wafers. Technicians maintain the equipment and check the chips for flaws.

SOMETHING EXTRA

Silicon Valley is not actually made out of silicon. It is the name given to the southern part of the San Francisco Bay area that became known for its creation of microchips. Silicon Valley has become synonymous with many high-tech products and inventions—and the people who got rich making them. The area continues to be one of the world's top research centers.

Subjects to Study

Math, physics, chemistry, computer science, electronics, shop

Discover More

To learn more about jobs as a semiconductor processor, write to the Maricopa Advanced Technology Education Center at 2323 West 14th St., Suite 540, Tempe, AZ 85281. Visit its Web site at http://matec.org/ops/career.shtml.

Related Jobs

Assemblers and fabricators; engineering technicians; engineers; inspectors, testers, sorters, samplers, and weighers; science technicians; tool and die makers

Education & Training
Voc/tech training

Earnings
$$$

Job Outlook
Declining

Transportation & Material Moving Occupations

Air Traffic Controllers

On the Job

Air traffic controllers are responsible for the safe movement of airport traffic both in the air and on the ground. Using radar and visual observation, they direct landings, takeoffs, and ground movement of aircraft. They keep planes a safe distance apart during flights and inform pilots of current weather conditions. In emergencies, they may search for missing aircraft. This can be a very stressful job.

SOMETHING EXTRA

Do you like computer games in which you have to keep track of many small, moving objects? Imagine the objects as real-life aircraft, carrying real human beings. Your job is to know where they are, ensure they remain safely apart, and stay aware of conditions that affect them. Air traffic controllers must be able to track several aircraft, monitor weather and traffic, and stay calm under extreme stress.

Subjects to Study

English, math, computer skills, physics, science, shop, technology, foreign languages, electronics, communication skills

Discover More

Look at current air traffic at major airports. Check out the National Air Traffic Controllers Association's Web site at www.natca.org.

Related Jobs

Aircraft pilots and flight engineers

Education & Training
Long-term OJT

Earnings
$$$$$

Job Outlook
Average increase

Aircraft Pilots & Flight Engineers

On the Job

Aircraft pilots fly airplanes and helicopters, test aircraft, and sometimes fight forest fires. Pilots may work for large airlines, charter services, the government, or private businesses. They must plan flights, check the aircraft and weather conditions, and keep records of each flight. Flight engineers act as a third pilot on large aircraft, monitoring and operating many instruments and systems.

SOMETHING EXTRA

U.S. Airways pilot Chesley Sullenberger became a hero in 2009 when he made an emergency landing on the Hudson River. Known as the "Miracle on the Hudson," the flight's passengers and crew all survived. Sullenberger got his pilot's license at 14, flew Air Force fighter jets, investigated air disasters, and even studied how pilots behave during crises. He was the right pilot in the right place at the right time.

Subjects to Study

English, math, computer skills, electronics, geography, physics

Discover More

If you are interested in exploring this career, consider Aviation Career Education (ACE) Camp. This camp is designed for middle and high school students and lasts from one day to one week. For more information, visit www.faa.gov.

Related Jobs

Air traffic controllers

Education & Training
Voc/tech training to Bachelor's degree

Earnings
$$$$$

Job Outlook
Average increase

Bus Drivers

On the Job

Bus drivers transport people from place to place following a schedule and a specific route. Some drive people long distances within a state or throughout the country. Others drive locally only. School bus drivers drive students to and from school. These workers deal with many passengers and heavy traffic, often in bad weather. Some work nights, weekends, and holidays. Others travel overnight away from their homes. Many school bus drivers work part-time.

SOMETHING EXTRA

Do you wear a seat belt on the school bus? Some states require that school buses be equipped with seat belts for all riders. Other states are studying the idea. Proponents say seat belts will protect kids in a crash. But others say seat belts will slow down the time it takes to evacuate the bus in an emergency. Either way, it's a timely debate. More than 23 million students ride school buses every day in America.

Subjects to Study

English, communication skills, math, driver's education, first aid

Discover More

Take a ride on a city bus and talk to the bus driver about this job. What tests does your state require? Is special training required? Watch what the driver does to communicate with passengers and care for the bus, but don't distract him or her too much.

Related Jobs

Rail transportation occupations, taxi drivers and chauffeurs, truck drivers and driver/sales workers

Education & Training
Moderate-term OJT

Earnings
$$

Job Outlook
Average increase

Taxi Drivers & Chauffeurs

On the Job

Taxi drivers and chauffeurs drive people in cars, limousines, and vans. Taxi drivers drive people to airports, hotels, or restaurants. Chauffeurs pamper their passengers by providing extras like newspapers, drinks, music, and television. These workers must lift heavy luggage and packages, drive in all kinds of weather and traffic, and sometimes put up with rude customers. Most taxi drivers and chauffeurs work nights and weekends.

SOMETHING EXTRA

Riding in a limousine is all about traveling in style. Many limos feature drink cabinets, mini-fridges, flat screen televisions, DVD players, and video-game systems, not to mention a ton of leg room and comfy leather interior. Some stretch limos provide hot tubs or Jacuzzis. With features like these, why get out of the car?

Subjects to Study

English, math, physical education, driver's education

Discover More

Take a taxi ride with a parent and talk to the driver. Ask about the best and worst parts of the job. Has he or she driven anyone famous?

Related Jobs

Bus drivers, truck drivers and driver/sales workers

Education & Training
Short-term OJT

Earnings
$

Job Outlook
Above-average increase

Truck Drivers & Driver/Sales Workers

On the Job

Truck drivers move and deliver goods between factories, terminals, warehouses, stores, and homes. They maintain their trucks, check for fuel and oil, make sure their brakes and lights work, and do minor repairs. They load and unload the goods they transport. They drive in heavy traffic and bad weather. Some self-employed truckers may spend 240 days a year on the road.

Subjects to Study

Math, driver's education, physical education, accounting

Discover More

Call a truck driver training school in your area. Ask whether you can visit the school and see the rigs they drive. Maybe an instructor will take you for a ride.

Related Jobs

Bus drivers; Postal Service mail carriers; sales representatives, wholesale and manufacturing; taxi drivers and chauffeurs

Education & Training
Short-term OJT

Earnings
$$$

Job Outlook
Average increase

Rail Transportation Occupations

On the Job

This job includes railroad workers as well as subway and streetcar operators. Railroad engineers operate locomotives that transport passengers and cargo. Conductors are responsible for the cargo and passengers on trains. Brakemen remove cars and throw switches to allow trains to change tracks. Railroads operate around the clock, seven days a week. Employees work nights, weekends, and holidays. Some spend several nights a week away from home.

SOMETHING EXTRA

In the late 1800s, when the railroad was the best way to travel, wealthy people sometimes bought their own railroad cars. These cars were usually decorated with rich, expensive materials. Some had luxury items such as sunken bathtubs, barber's chairs, and pipe organs. When they wanted to travel, these wealthy folks had their cars hitched to a train and traveled in style. Most employed their own maids, chefs, and waiters to serve them on the trip.

Subjects to Study

Math, geography, driver's education, physical education

Discover More

Visit a railroad station or ride a train or subway and watch the different workers. If they have free time, ask them about their jobs. What are the best and worst parts? Do they get to ride for free when they are off-duty?

Related Jobs

Bus drivers, heavy vehicle and mobile equipment service technicians and mechanics, material moving occupations, truck drivers and driver/sales workers, water transportation occupations

Education & Training
Moderate-term OJT

Earnings
$$$$

Job Outlook
Average increase

Water Transportation Occupations

On the Job

Workers in water transportation operate all kinds of boats on oceans, the Great Lakes, rivers, canals, and other waterways. Captains or masters are in charge of a vessel and the crew. Deck officers or mates help the captain. Seamen and deck hands do maintenance, steer, and load and unload cargo. Pilots guide ships through harbors and narrow waterways. These workers are outdoors in all kinds of weather. Many spend long periods away from home.

SOMETHING EXTRA

Merchant mariners working on ships on the Great Lakes typically work for 60 days straight and then have 30 days off. These long cruises involve hard work and offer little job security. Most sailors are hired for one voyage at a time. During the winter months when the lakes are frozen, there is no work at all. So why do they do it? Most work these jobs simply because they love being on the water.

Subjects to Study

Math, physical education, swimming, first aid

Discover More

Water transportation workers must be comfortable both on and in the water. Take swimming lessons at your local park or YMCA. Then sign up for a water-safety or first-aid course.

Related Jobs

Fishers and fishing vessel operators, heavy vehicle and mobile equipment service technicians and mechanics, job opportunities in the armed forces

Education & Training
Short-term OJT to Work experience

Earnings
$$$$

Job Outlook
Above-average increase

Material Moving Occupations

On the Job

Material moving equipment operators and laborers load and unload trucks and ships using cranes, bulldozers, and forklifts. They move construction materials, logs, and coal around factories, warehouses, and construction sites. They sometimes set up, clean, and repair equipment. Most work outdoors in all kinds of weather. Others work inside warehouses or factories. The machinery may be noisy and dangerous.

SOMETHING EXTRA

Crane safety is a big concern. Many cranes operate on a construction site. In 2004, a crane collapsed on a Toledo interstate highway, killing four people. That's why cranes are inspected regularly, and operators receive special safety training.

Subjects to Study

Shop, auto mechanics, driver's education, first aid

Discover More

Look for material moving machines in your community. What do they move? Are they used in any work except construction? How do the operators control the machines?

Related Jobs

Agricultural workers, other; building cleaning workers; construction equipment operators; construction laborers; grounds maintenance workers; logging workers

Education & Training
Short-term OJT to Long-term OJT

Earnings
$

Job Outlook
Declining

Job Opportunities in the Armed Forces

Job Opportunities in the Armed Forces

On the Job

The U.S. armed forces is the country's largest employer. Maintaining a strong defense requires many activities, such as running hospitals, repairing helicopters, programming computers, and operating nuclear reactors. Military jobs range from clerical work to professional positions to construction work.

People in the military must serve for a specified time and can be moved from one base to another. Many work nights, weekends, and holidays. Combat duty is always possible.

SOMETHING EXTRA

What jobs does military training prepare you for? Almost anything. The armed forces train doctors, nurses, journalists, surveyors, meteorologists, computer specialists, pilots, sailors, electronics equipment repairers, mechanics, and craft workers. Many employers like hiring former military personnel because they know about discipline, honor, and getting the job done.

Subjects to Study

Math, English, business, science courses, shop, physical education

Discover More

Do you think you would enjoy military life? Talk to people who have served in the armed forces. Contact a recruiter to find out about a branch of the military. (Remember, though, that a recruiter's job is to get people to join.) Check the Military Careers Web site at www.militarycareers.com to learn about specific jobs, as well as information about all five branches of the military (Army, Navy, Air Force, Marines, Coast Guard).

Education & Training
Moderate-term OJT to Work experience

Earnings
$$$

Job Outlook
Little change

Related Jobs

Nearly any civilian job

Young Person's Occupational Outlook Handbook, © JIST Works

Appendix

More Job Information on the Web

The Internet is a great place to find out more about jobs that interest you. Here are some Web sites that will get you started.

General Career Exploration and Reference

Occupational Outlook Handbook
www.bls.gov/oco

O*NET Online
http://online.onetcenter.org

America's Career InfoNet
www.acinet.org/acinet

Career Guide to Industries
www.bls.gov/oco/cg

Career Voyages
www.careervoyages.gov

JobProfiles.org
www.jobprofiles.org

JIST Publishing
www.jist.com

Green Occupations

American Wind Energy Association
www.awea.org

Biodiesel Jobs
www.biodiesel-jobs.com

Energy Star
www.energystar.gov

Ethanol Jobs
www.ethanol-jobs.com

Geothermal Energy Association
www.geo-energy.org

Interstate Renewable Energy Council
www.irecusa.org

National Hydropower Association
www.hydro.org

Renewable Fuels Association
www.ethanolrfa.org

Residential Energy Services Network
www.resnet.us

Solar Energy International
www.solarenergy.org

Management & Business & Financial Occupations

American Association of Advertising Agencies
www.aaaa.org

American Board of Funeral Services Education
www.abfse.org

American College of Health Care Administrators
www.achca.org

American Council for Construction Education
www.acce-hq.org

American Institute of Certified Public Accountants
www.aicpa.org

American Management Association
www.amanet.org

American Purchasing Society
www.american-purchasing.com

American Society of Farm Managers and Rural Appraisers
www.asfmra.org

Association for the Advancement of Cost Engineering
www.aacei.org

Association of Higher Education Facilities Officers
www.appa.org

Association of Management Consulting Firms
www.amcf.org

Association of University Programs in Health Administration
www.aupha.org

Community Associations Institute
www.caionline.org

Financial Management Association International
www.fma.org

Financial Planning Association
www.fpanet.org

Institute of Certified Professional Managers
www.icpm.biz

Institute of Internal Auditors
www.theiia.org

Institute of Real Estate Management
www.irem.org

Insurance Information Institute
www.iii.org

Insurance Institute of America
www.aicpcu.org

International Claim Association
www.claim.org

International Council on Hotel, Restaurant, and Institutional Education
www.chrie.org

International Facility Management Association
www.ifma.org

Mortgage Bankers Association of America
www.mbaa.org

National Association of Elementary School Principals
www.naesp.org

National Association of Secondary School Principals
www.nassp.org

National Association of State Budget Officers
www.nasbo.org

National Funeral Directors Association
www.nfda.org

National Restaurant Association Educational Foundation
www.nraef.org

Society for Human Resource Management
www.shrm.org

Professional & Related Occupations

Aerospace Industries Association
www.aia-aerospace.org

Alliance of Cardiovascular Professionals
www.acp-online.org

American Academy of Actuaries
www.actuary.org

American Academy of Environmental Engineers
www.aaee.net

American Academy of Forensic Sciences
www.aafs.org

American Academy of Physician Assistants Information Center
www.aapa.org

American Anthropological Association
www.aaanet.org

American Association for Laboratory Animal Science
www.aalas.org

American Association for Respiratory Care
www.aarc.org

American Association of Bioanalysts
www.aab.org

American Association of Colleges of Pharmacy
www.aacp.org

American Association of Petroleum Geologists
www.aapg.org

American Association of Pharmaceutical Scientists
www.aaps.org

American Bar Association
www.abanet.org

American Chemical Society
www.acs.org

American Congress on Surveying and Mapping
www.acsm.net

American Correctional Association
www.aca.org

American Counseling Association
www.counseling.org

American Dental Association
www.ada.org

American Design Drafting Association
www.adda.org

American Dietetic Association
www.eatright.org

American Geological Institute
www.agiweb.org

American Health Information
Management Association
www.ahima.org

American Historical Association
www.historians.org

American Institute of Architects
www.aia.org

American Institute of Biological Sciences
www.aibs.org

American Institute of Chemical
Engineers
www.aiche.org

American Institute of Graphic Arts
www.aiga.org

American Institute of Physics
www.aip.org

American Library Association
www.ala.org

American Mathematical Society
www.ams.org

American Meteorological Society
www.ametsoc.org

American Nuclear Society
www.ans.org

American Occupational Therapy
Association
www.aota.org

American Physical Society
www.aps.org

American Physical Therapy Association
www.apta.org

American Planning Association
www.planning.org

American Podiatric Medical Association
www.apma.org

American Political Science Association
www.apsanet.org

American Probation and Parole
Association
www.appa-net.org

American Psychological Association
www.apa.org

American Society for Clinical Pathology
www.ascp.org

American Society for Engineering
Education
www.asee.org

American Society for Microbiology
www.asm.org

American Society of Agricultural
Engineers
www.asaecenter.org

American Society of Agronomy
www.agronomy.org

American Society of Civil Engineers
www.asce.org

American Society of Health-System
Pharmacists
www.ashp.org

American Society of Landscape
Architects
www.asla.org

American Society of Mechanical
Engineers
www.asme.org

American Society of Radiologic
Technologist
www.asrt.org

American Society of Safety Engineers
www.asse.org

American Sociological Association
www.asanet.org

American Speech-Language-Hearing
Association
www.asha.org

American Statistical Association
www.amstat.org

American Therapeutic Recreation
Association
www.atra-tr.org

American Translators Association
www.atanet.org

American Veterinary Medical
Association
www.avma.org

Archaeological Institute of America
www.archaeological.org

Association for Career and Technical
Education
www.acteonline.org

Association for Computing Machinery
www.acm.org

Association of American Colleges and
Universities
www.aacu.org

Association of American Geographers
www.aag.org

Association of American Medical
Colleges
www.aamc.org

Association of Schools and Colleges of
Optometry
www.opted.org

Association of Surgical Technologists
www.ast.org

Biomedical Engineering Society
www.bmes.org

Council of American Survey Research
Organizations
www.casro.org

Council on Chiropractic Education
www.cce-usa.org

Division of Education, American Dental
Hygienists' Association
www.adha.org

Institute for Operations Research and
Management Science
www.informs.org

Institute of Electrical and Electronics Engineers
www.ieee.org

Institute of Electrical and Electronics Engineers Computer Society
www.computer.org

Institute of Industrial Engineers
www.iienet.org

Junior Engineering Technical Society
www.jets.org

Marketing Research Association
www.mra-net.org

Materials Research Society
www.mrs.org

Minerals, Metals, & Material Society
www.tms.org

National Accrediting Agency for Clinical Laboratory Sciences
www.naacls.org

National Association for Business Economics
www.nabe.com

National Association for Practical Nurse Education and Service
www.napnes.org

National Association for the Education of Young Children
www.naeyc.org

National Association of Broadcasters
www.nab.org

National Association of Emergency Medical Technicians
www.naemt.org

National Association of Legal Assistants
www.nala.org

National Association of Schools of Art and Design
http://nasad.arts-accredit.org

National Association of Schools of Music
http://nasm.arts-accredit.org

National Association of Schools of Public Affairs and Administration
www.naspaa.org

National Association of Schools of Theater
http://nast.arts-accredit.org

National Association of Social Workers
www.socialworkers.org

National Center for State Courts
www.ncsconline.org

National Court Reporters Association
www.ncraonline.org

National Federation of Paralegal Associations
www.paralegals.org

National High School Athletic Coaches Association
www.hscoaches.org

National League of Nursing
www.nln.org

National Organization for Human Service Education
www.nationalhumanservices.org

National Workforce Center for Emerging Technologies
www.nwcet.org

Pharmacy Technician Certification Board
www.ptcb.org

Professional Photographers of America
www.ppa.com

Public Relations Society of America
www.prsa.org

Society for American Archaeology
www.saa.org

Society for Mining, Metallurgy and Exploration
www.smenet.org

Society for Technical Communication
www.stc.org

Society of American Archivists
www.archivists.org

Society of Broadcast Engineers
www.sbe.org

Society of Diagnostic Medical Sonography
www.sdms.org

Society of Nuclear Medicine
www.snm.org

Society of Petroleum Engineers
www.spe.org

U.S. Department of Education, Office of Vocational and Adult Education
www.ed.gov/about/offices/list/ovae

U.S. Department of Labor, Occupational Safety and Health Administration
www.osha.gov

Service Occupations

American Association of Medical Assistants
www.aama-ntl.org

American Association for Medical Transcription
www.aamt.org

American Council on Exercise
www.acefitness.org

American Dental Assistants Association
www.dentalassistant.org

American Gaming Association
www.americangaming.org

American Jail Association
www.corrections.com/aja

Association of American Pesticide Control Officials
http://aapco.ceris.purdue.edu

Federal Bureau of Investigation
www.fbi.gov

Humane Society of the United States
www.humanesociety.org

International Association of Firefighters
www.iaff.org

International Executive Housekeepers Association
www.ieha.org

National Animal Control Association
www.nacanet.org

National Association for Home Care
www.nahc.org

National Cosmetology Association
www.salonprofessionals.org

National Dog Groomers Association of America
www.nationaldoggroomers.com

National Restaurant Association
www.restaurant.org

Tree Care Industry Association
www.treecareindustry.org

Sales & Related Occupations

American Rental Association
www.ararental.org

American Society of Travel Agents
www.astanet.com

Independent Insurance Agents of America
www.iiaba.net

International Foodservice Distributors Association
www.ifdaonline.org

Manufacturers' Agents National Association
www.manaonline.org

Manufacturers' Representatives Educational Research Foundation
www.mrerf.org

National Association of Health Underwriters
www.nahu.org

National Association of Realtors
www.realtor.org

National Automobile Dealers Association
www.nada.org

National Retail Federation
www.nrf.com

Retail, Wholesale, and Department Store Union
www.rwdsu.org

Securities Industry and Financial Markets Association
www.sifma.org

Office & Administrative Support Occupations

Air Transport Association of America
www.airlines.org

American Institute of Professional Bookkeepers
www.aipb.org

Association of Computer Operations Management
www.afcom.com

Association of Credit and Collection Professionals
www.acainternational.org

Association of Public Safety Communications Officials
www.apco911.org

Association for Suppliers of Printing, Publishing and Converting Technologies
www.npes.org/education/index.html

Communications Workers of America
www.cwa-union.org

Council on Library/Media Technicians
http://colt.ucr.edu

Education Institute of the American Hotel and Lodging Association
www.ei-ahla.org

International Association of Administrative Professionals
www.iaap-hq.org

Legal Secretaries International
www.legalsecretaries.org

National Academies of Emergency Dispatch
www.emergencydispatch.org

National Management Association
www.nma1.org

United States Postal Service
www.usps.com/about

Farming, Fishing & Forestry Occupations

American Forest & Paper Association
www.afandpa.org

Forest Resources Association
www.forestresources.org

Marine Technology Society
www.mtsociety.org

National FFA Organization
www.ffa.org

New England Small Farm Institute
www.smallfarm.org

Society of American Foresters
www.safnet.org

U.S. Forest Service
www.fs.fed.us

Construction Trades & Related Workers

American Society of Home Inspectors
www.ashi.org

Associated General Contractors of America
www.agc.org

Associated of Construction Inspectors
www.aci-assoc.org

Brotherhood of Boilermakers
www.boilermakers.org

Floor Covering Installation Contractors Association
www.fcica.com

International Association of Bridge, Structural, Ornamental, and Reinforcing Iron Workers
www.ironworkers.org

International Association of Electrical Inspectors
www.iaei.org

International Masonry Institute
www.imiweb.org

International Union of Elevator Constructors
www.iuec.org

International Union of Operating Engineers
www.iuoe.org

International Union of Painters and Allied Trades
www.iupat.org

Laborers' International Union of North America
www.liuna.org

Laborers—AGC Education and Training Fund
www.laborerslearn.org

National Association of Home Builders
www.nahb.org

National Association of Plumbing-Heating-Cooling Contractors
www.phccweb.org

National Center for Construction Education and Research
www.nccer.org

National Concrete Masonry Association
www.ncma.org

National Electrical Contractors Association
www.necanet.org

National Glass Association
www.glass.org

National Insulation Association
www.insulation.org

National Joint Apprenticeship Training Committee
www.njatc.org

National Roofing Contractors Association
www.nrca.net

Operative Plasterers' and Cement Masons' International Association of the United States and Canada

www.opcmia.org

Painting and Decorating Contractors of America

www.pdca.org

Sheet Metal Workers International Association

www.smwia.org

United Brotherhood of Carpenters and Joiners of America

www.carpenters.org

Installation, Maintenance & Repair Occupations

ACES International (Fiber Optics, Electronics, and Communications Professionals

www.acesinternational.org

Air-Conditioning Contractors of America

www.acca.org

Association of Equipment Management Professionals

www.aemp.org

Automotive Service Association

www.asashop.org

Automotive Youth Educational Systems

www.ayes.org

Computing Technology Industry Association

www.comptia.org

Custom Electronic Design and Installation Association

www.cedia.net

International Brotherhood of Electrical Workers

www.ibew.org

Instrumentation, Systems, and Automation Society

www.isa.org

National Automatic Merchandising Association

www.vending.org

National Tooling and Machining Association

www.ntma.org

Professional Aviation Maintenance Association

www.pama.org

SkillsUSA

www.skillsusa.org

Production Occupations

American Public Power Association
www.appanet.org

American Society for Quality
www.asq.org

American Water Works Association
www.awwa.org

American Welding Society
www.aws.org

National Association of Dental Laboratories
www.nadl.org

Precision Machine Products Association
www.pmpa.org

Precision Metalforming Association Educational Foundation
www.pmaef.org

Semiconductor Industry Association
www.sia-online.org

Woodworker's Central
www.woodworking.org

Transportation & Material Moving Occupations

Air Line Pilots Association
www.alpa.org

American Public Transportation Association
www.apta.com

American Trucking Association
www.truckline.com

Association of American Railroads
www.aar.org

Federal Aviation Administration
www.faa.gov

National Limousine Association
www.limo.org

United Motorcoach Association
www.uma.org

Job Opportunities in the Armed Forces

Military Career Guide Online
www.todaysmilitary.com

Index